SOCIOLOGY, EQUALITY AND EDUCATION

SOCIOLOGY, EQUALITY AND EDUCATION

Philosophical Essays in Defense of a
Variety of Differences

ANTONY FLEW

Professor of Philosophy
University of Reading

BOOKS
10 East 53d St., New York 10022
(a division of Harper & Row Publishers, Inc.)

First published in the United Kingdom
1976 by The Macmillan Press Ltd

Published in the U.S.A. 1976 by
HARPER & ROW PUBLISHERS, INC.
BARNES & NOBLE IMPORT DIVISION

ISBN 0-06-492118-2

Printed in Great Britain

Contents

Acknowledgements

The author and publisher wish to thank the following for agreeing to publication here in revised form of material previously published: Mr Hector Hawton, Editor of *Question* ('Reality, Rationality and the Possibility of Anthropology', *Question Five*, 1972; 'Sociology and Equality', *Question Eight*, 1975); Mr Renford Bambrough, Editor of *Philosophy* ('The Jensen Uproar', *Philosophy*, 1973); Professor Jonas F. Soltis, President of the Philosophy of Education Society, and Professor Brian Crittenden, Editor of the Proceedings of the Twenty-Ninth Meeting of that society ('Teaching and Testing', *Philosophy of Education 1973*); Sir Anthony Meyer, M.P., sometime Editor of *Solon* ('Principles and Participation', *Solon*, 1969).

Foreword

This collection of papers by Professor Flew is both theoretical and practical in its import. Its central concern is education; its dominant note, a plea for rationality in our approach to that subject. What constitutes rationality, and how education should be conducted in order to conform to it, are matters on which the author has strong views. Students of the philosophy of education will appreciate the clear manner in which he relates his contribution to that subject to certain basic issues in the philosophy of the social sciences; those actively involved in education will, I imagine, react vigorously to Professor Flew's cogently voiced opinions on the present practice of education. His own introductory chapter shows the scope of the book and gives an indication how theoretical and practical concerns are to be interwoven within it.

University of Exeter   W. D. HUDSON

1 Where We Are Going

This is a selection of essays in the philosophy of education. Some friends, and indeed some enemies, even without my suggestion would describe it as a one-man volume of philosophical *Black Papers*. But it certainly is not an idle and uncomplicated reprinting in new book form of work already once published somewhere else. For nearly half the material is quite fresh, while all the rest has been revised more or less drastically. Nor are all the chapters essays in the philosophy of education, and nothing else. This exclusive characterisation is tolerably apt for the three chapters in Part Two. But the four in the longer Part One have an equally strong claim to rate as contributions to the philosophy of the social sciences.

What, however, gives the whole selection unity is a concern for educational standards; and a commitment to defend these standards against an educationally destructive new egalitarianism. This new egalitarianism, which I shall in Chapter 6 be contrasting with some other and more admirable ideals of equality, requires us to conceal, or to devalue, or even to deny, differences in individual talent and temperament and achievement. It minimises or outright rejects all qualitative distinctions between cultures, whether these be the cultures of different societies or of different persons or groups within the same society. The notion of objective knowledge falls under the same ban: were this to be allowed it might serve as a basis for discrimination between superior and inferior. There is opposition to any form of testing which reveals, and may perhaps encourage, differences in educational achievement. Since there can on these principles be no real and relevant difference between those qualified to teach and those still under instruction, there are demands that students should have a, if not the, deciding voice in the appointment of teachers and in the design of courses of study – demands which are today often urged in the name of academic freedom.

Part Two deals with some of these claims presented without theoretical backing. Chapter 6, 'Teaching and Testing', argues that in order to be sincerely trying to teach, or trying to learn, people must be ready to monitor their progress: some form of assessment or examination, but not any one particular form, is essential to intentional education – not merely as a matter of fact but as a matter of logic. Chapter 7, 'Principles and Participation', insists upon elementary distinctions needed for fundamental discussion of the practical issues of student participation in the government of institutions of tertiary education. Chapter 8, 'Academic Freedoms and Academic Purposes', argues that any special case for distinctively academic freedoms must be based upon the peculiarities of academic functions and academic purposes. It has to refer to the nature of truth-concerned critical inquiry. It certainly cannot afford to despise or depreciate knowledge, academic discipline, or academic qualifications.

Part One treats various misreadings of the implications and presuppositions of social sciences, misreadings which are today at work providing support for some or all the tendencies just now colligated as the new egalitarianism. The longest chapter, 'Metaphysical Idealism and the Sociology of Knowledge', comprehends almost the whole collection. For the central misconception here is that to be able to ask sociological questions about the forces involved in recognising and maintaining distinctions made in education, is to show that these distinctions themselves are problematic, and to give reason to believe that they are without foundation in any real, objective differences. I hope that I succeed in demonstrating that the achievements and aspirations of sociology in general, and of the sociology of knowledge in particular, neither presuppose nor imply anything of the sort. On the contrary: the denial of the possibility of objective knowledge, and the new brand of philosophical idealism, which are both offered as elements in a sociological revelation, are in fact altogether inconsistent with any science of sociology.

Chapter 3, 'Reality, Rationality and the Possibility of Anthropology', confronts standardless relativism: the notion that the 'science' of the Azande, for instance, cannot properly be said to involve any falsehood or irrationality, since these would then be attributed only by your or our, not by Azande, criteria of truth and rationality. It is, it is assumed, naive and pre-Kuhnian to suggest that a theory might be criticised, and even shown to be false, by reference to objective realities in the universe around us: "the assumption that there exists a realm of facts independent of theories which establish their meaning is fundamentally unscientific" (Cockburn and Blackburn, p. 10).

I hope that I succeed here again in demonstrating not only that these educationally subversive ideas are neither presupposed nor implied by the studies which are thought to support them, but also that they are actually incompatible with the very possibility of either anthropology or the historiography of science. The outcome of Chapter 4, 'Sociology and Equality', is somewhat less drastic. The aim there is to reveal, and by that to neutralise, powerful occupational temptations. These occupational temptations frequently seduce both professional sociologists and the general sociological public into believing both that people naturally are, and that ideally they ought to be, more equal than actually is the case. The threat to the science itself is here far less total. But I can and do cite one or two of far too many examples of sociological work vitiated by the unstated, unrecognised, and in fact false assumption that natural endowments are equally distributed among all individuals and all social groups.

The misunderstandings of possible psychological findings attacked in Chapter 5, 'The Jensen Uproar', threaten psychology itself in a different way. In this case the viciously uncomprehending hullabaloo raised against those who have dared to produce evidence of average differences in natural endowments as between different racial groups must obviously discourage free inquiry in this area. There are good grounds for believing that this is actually happening in the United States: grant-awarding bodies refuse to finance such dangerous and heretical research; while some of those with excellent professional reasons to conclude that there in fact are differences of this kind privately confess that they have been intimidated into public silence (Jensen, p. 330; and the Preface passim, but especially pp. 46-8).

The tone of the present book is often rather more vehement than is usual in philosophy, while the last two chapters make some fairly sharp and specific political references. One or two of these references will, I know well, touch off reflex thought-stopping cries: 'Cold Warrior'; 'sterile anti-Communism'; even 'reds under the bed' (Flew: 7, §§ 4.23, 5.1). Yet I shall not recant either the occasional strong words or these unfashionable political references. They are, I think, all argumentatively warranted and to the point.

When, for instance, a Secretary of State for Education and Science goes out of his way to tell a conference of the Association of Education Committees that much of what our universities provide for our students is "intellectual junk", and when the same person both in Parliament and elsewhere makes attacks on university government, confounding the most elementary and fundamental distinctions; then, surely, it becomes relevant in discussing 'Principles and Participation' in such government to make some passing reference to these ministerial contributions? Again, when a spokesman for a Council for Academic Freedom and Democracy, in a work sponsored by that Council, makes a point of commending one of his Muscovite Communist colleagues for splendid labours to prevent defence research in British universities; then, surely, it would be culpably unrealistic not to remark that these activities have much more to do with the removal of obstacles to the further expansion of the Soviet Empire than with the extension of academic freedom or any sort of democracy?

As for the occasional strong words, here and elsewhere, they are appropriate to the importance of the educational and liberal values being threatened. The creature which responds to attacks with the same vigour as is shown by the attackers is not wicked but simply robust. Faced by that new sociological idealism, to be examined in Chapter 2, I recall some of the no less vehement words used about 'Toynbee the Prophet' by that admirable Dutch scholar and patriot Pieter Geyl: "I feel an irrepressible urge to testify against this false witness . . . and oppose a system productive of such pernicious counsels" (Geyl, p. 163). Again, when challenged by standardless relativism, the doctrine to be examined in Chapter 3, I think of the commendation of "gloves off philosophy" in the final pages of the *Autobiography* of an older Oxford philosopher: this disastrous doctrine "means the end of clear thinking and the triumph of irrationalism" (Collingwood, p. 112).

The bibliographical history of the remaining seven papers in the present volume follows. 'Metaphysical Idealism and the Sociology of Knowledge' is a virgin. Sections 1 and 3 of 'Reality,

Rationality and the Possibility of Anthropology' are equally new; but Section 2 is based on 'Anthropology and Rationality', which appeared in *Question Five*, published by Pemberton of London in 1972. 'Sociology and Equality' is a revised and slightly extended version of an article under the same title first printed in *Question Eight* in 1975: *Question*, by the way, is the successor of the old *Rationalist Annual.* 'The Jensen Uproar' incorporates material from several previously published sources: the main source was a discussion note under the same title in *Philosophy* for 1973; but I also drew on my rejoinder to two critics in *Philosophy* for 1974, on letters and a short article in the *Times Higher Education Supplement* in 1973, and on three reviews for the *Spectator* in 1972. The first version of 'Teaching and Testing' was read to the New Orleans conference of the Philosophy of Education Society in 1973, and first published by them. 'Principles and Participation' was in the first issue of the since defunct journal *Solon* in 1969. (The Acknowledgements on p. vi above give formal expression of my thanks to the individuals and societies concerned, but I should like to say again here how much I appreciate their permission to redeploy material previously published.)

The final essay, 'Academic Freedoms and Academic Purposes', has never been in print before. Thereby hangs a tale. For the original rather shorter version was commissioned for inclusion in *Black Paper 1975*. In accepting it the Editor wrote: "I am delighted with your article. It is most forceful and exactly what we want." When, however, the publishers received the complete typescript for the whole volume they decided, against editorial protest, to excise my contribution. The explanation which they offered to me was, simply, that "it was inappropriate in the context of the other *Black Paper* articles". Happily book publishing in Britain has not yet been turned into a state monopoly, and the article – which has lost no force in the consequent revision – now appears in a different volume under a different imprint. It is, you might say, a black paper which was itself once 'blacked'!

Part One

2 Metaphysical Idealism and the Sociology of Knowledge

1. *Materialism and Sociologico-criticism*

I shall in the present chapter be dealing with a collection of papers on *Knowledge and Control*. The cover proclaims this to be an Open University Set Book. The selection was made and edited by Michael F. D. Young, who since receiving his M.A. from Essex has been a Lecturer in Sociology at the University of London Institute of Education. These two institutional facts must have guaranteed a wide circulation; and, as I originally learned from Richard Peters, whom I now thank for first drawing my attention to the book, its characteristic notions are indeed much in vogue, not only in Institutes and Colleges of Education, but also in the school staff-rooms from which the Open University draws so many of its clients.

These characteristic notions, which I propose to examine, do not of course exhaust the contents of the book. But it is they which appear to be most, and most damagingly, influential. It is they too about which a philosopher in his professional capacity can have something useful to say. Yet in fairness we must be careful not to hold all the contributors equally responsible for these notions. The book contains, for instance, two papers by Pierre Bourdieu of the École Pratique des Hautes Études at the Sorbonne. Neither of these is marred by the tendencies to which I take exception. Both belong as much to the history of ideas as to the sociology of knowledge; and the second, an examination of the enormous effectiveness of the French educational system in shaping French intellectual life, is a model of how such studies can be illuminating both to practising teachers and to teachers in training.[1] On the other hand we cannot say in Young's defence that he did not know what he was going to find himself sponsoring. For of the only two contributions other than his own which had not been published previously one is by Basil Bernstein, Young's Head of Department, while the other, by Geoffrey Esland of the Open University, was distilled from a London M.A. thesis apparently done under Young's supervision.

The tendencies which I am going to pick out, and to attack, can be seen as in one aspect tendencies towards a sociological version of metaphysical idealism. The meaning of the word 'idealism' in the present context is best explained by quoting from V. I. Lenin's *Materialism and Empirio-Criticism*. The idealist Berkeley, says Lenin, "bluntly defines the viewpoint of his opponents as being that they recognize the thing-in-itself. . . . 'the absolute existence of sensible objects, in themselves, or without the mind'. . . . The two fundamental lines of philosophical outlook are here depicted with the straightforwardness, clarity and precision that distinguish the classical philosophers. . . . Materialism is the recognition of objects in themselves . . . outside the mind. . . . The opposite doctrine [idealism] claims that objects do not exist 'without the mind' " (Lenin, p. 17).

I cite these two definitions from a Marxist rather than a 'bourgeois' source partly – as their trade jargon has it – in order to legitimate myself in the eyes of the sociologists. But the main aim of several such references, direct or oblique, both here and in the following chapter, to Lenin's remarkable essay, is to underscore resemblances, both between empirio-criticism and this new sociologico-criticism, and between Lenin's polemic against the former and mine against the latter. Lenin, however, lost interest once the class enemy was exposed as false, idealist, and un-Marxist. I am, by contrast, as befits a philosopher, also concerned to recognise and to neutralise the sources of error.

The empirio-critics were the precursors before the First World War of the Vienna Circle between the wars. Ernst Mach and Richard Avenarius, and in our own country Karl Pearson, like their successors the Logical Positivists, thought of themselves as hardheaded and this-worldly spokesmen for a through and through scientific world-outlook. Nevertheless, Lenin urged, covertly and by implication their position was not merely idealistic but solipsistic, and hence wholly irreconcilable both with the discoveries of science and with the facts of common experience: "If bodies are 'complexes of sensations', as Mach says, or 'combinations of sensations', as Berkeley said, it inevitably follows that the whole world is but my idea. Starting from such a premise it is impossible to arrive at the existence of other people besides oneself. It is the purest solipsism" (Lenin, p. 34).

The 'Introduction' to *Knowledge and Control* declares Young's intentions: "The primary aim of this book is to open up some alternative and, it is hoped, fruitful directions for sociological enquiry in education" (p. 2); above all "sociology of education is no longer conceived as an area of enquiry distinct from the sociology of knowledge" (p. 3). So we must "explore the implications of treating knowledge, or 'what counts as know-ledge', as socially constituted or constructed" (p. 5), insisting that "the subversion of absolutism by sociology is of crucial importance for the sociology of education" (p. 6). Wright Mills is thus quoted as suggesting "that the rules of logic, whether practical or academic, are conventional. . . . If logic, 'good reasoning', asking questions, and all the various sets of activities prescribed for the learner are conceived from one perspective as sets of social conventions which have meanings common to the prescribers, then the failure to comply with the prescriptions can be conceived, not as in the everyday world of the teacher as 'wrong', 'bad spelling or grammar', or 'poorly argued and expressed', but as forms of deviance . . . Thus the direction of research for the sociology of educational knowledge becomes to explore how and why certain dominant categories persist, and the nature of their possible links to sets of interests or activities such as occupational groupings" (pp. 5-6).

So far, perhaps, so good; so far, that is, as all this is construed only as recommending investigations of what interests or groupings support or inhibit what – altogether without preju-dice to any questions about the merits or demerits of whatever happens to be thus supported or inhibited. But the necessary limitation is never, I think, explicitly recognised in *Knowledge and Control.* Certainly the possibility of providing some sociologi-cal account of the interests supporting or opposing the making of some particular sort of discrimination is again and again misconstrued as a demonstration that there cannot be any real objective basis for such discriminations, that there are no corresponding discriminable differences 'without the mind'.

The most forthright, general, and extreme statement of such

sociological idealism comes as the conclusion of Alan Blum's article 'The Corpus of Knowledge'. Blum teaches at New York University. He writes: "it is easy to see that the methodical character of marriage, war and suicide is only seen, recognized and made possible through the organized practices of sociology. These regularities do not exist 'out there' in [a] pristine form to which sociologists functionally respond, but rather, they acquire their character of regularities and their features as describable objects only through the grace of sociological imputation. Thus, it is not an objectively discernible purely existing external world which accounts for sociology; it is the methods and procedures of sociology which create and sustain that world" (p. 131).

2.   *Sociological Insights and Metaphysical Idealism*

It helps to start with a statement like that, at once forthright, general, and extreme. But my own chief concern – and whatever importance the present exercise may have – lies in those tacit, partial and inhibited tendencies in the same direction which are found in many others who might, very understandably, shrink from a commitment so total as Blum's. Such tendencies are both the more common and the more dangerous precisely because they are much less obviously preposterous.

(i) Blum himself offers no warrant for accepting so breathtaking a conclusion. My own first ætiological conjecture is that it springs in part from a preposterous methodological confusion. Remember that there are many distinctively human ongoings in which it is impossible to engage unless you possess the relevant concepts. Examples are: planning to get married; joining up as a soldier; or committing suicide. For it would be incoherent to say of anyone that they were doing any of these things while you simultaneously insisted that they were not seized of the guiding and constitutive notions which are essential to these various activities. In all such cases – and they include everything distinctively human in human life – a mastery of the appropriate organising concepts must, of course, be a necessary condition of achieving any sociological understanding.

The subsistence of this class of distinctively human ongoings, and of their corresponding organising concepts, is a fact of fundamental importance for grasping the peculiarities of historiography, sociology, and the other human sciences.

Nevertheless it must be in the most literal sense preposterous to see this fundamental fact as a reason for holding – what is manifestly false – that "the methodical character of marriage, war and suicide is only . . . made possible through the organized practices of sociology". Nor is the consequential fact that certain things can be truly said only of people who possess some relevant concepts, a good reason for maintaining that these things cannot even be true of anyone until someone else turns up actually to make the appropriate assertions – that indispensable someone else being, of course, a sociologist equipped with those same essential organising concepts.

Blum offers his paradox as an answer to his own curiously Kantian question: 'How is sociology possible?' Yet it must be a basic precondition of the existence of sociology as a science that there are people – or, as Blum prefers to say, "societal members" – capable of doing their own social things, without benefit of sociologists and their imputations. It must be: just as much as it is a basic precondition of the existence of the science of the heavens that the stars in their courses exist and revolve in their own right, and are not mere creatures or fictions of the Astronomer Royal. The truth is flat contrary to what Blum asserts: there has to be, as there is, "an objectively discernible, purely existing external world which accounts for sociology". It cannot be, and it is not, "the methods and procedures of sociology which create and sustain that world".

(ii) A second, and perhaps more obvious, ætiological suggestion is that Blum is enormously exaggerating the extent of another phenomenon which is, I think, already real; and which is likely, if sociology continues to be the great boom subject, to become increasingly important. In so far as there can be and are, as there are, human activities which are essentially concept organised, in the way indicated in the previous section, it becomes possible, and indeed likely, that concepts originally created by sociologists, at least ostensibly in the interests of scientific understanding, will break out of the rather uncloistered cloisters of Departments of Sociology, and will be adopted by "societal members" as organising concepts, guiding and structuring both their own activities and their own understanding or misunderstanding of these activities.

There can be no doubt but that literature, plays and films do often have an effect of this sort. The boys go to the latest John

Wayne movie, and for the next week it is tall in the saddle all round the block. Adults read Kafka, and soon see themselves as Joseph K., to some extent modifying their conduct accordingly. Similarly a Weberian ideal type, originally offered as a tool of neutral and non-participatory understanding, may become the normative ideal of members of some particular society, and may in this or some other way guide both their social activities and their understanding of these activities. If we count Marx as among other things a sociologist, as we surely must, then the textbook example of this second phenomenon becomes the ever-growing influence of Marx's sociological ideas upon non-sociologists. Yet however far this influence, and this second phenomenon, extends now, or in the future will extend, it still remains true that sociology as a science presupposes the ontologically prior activities of "societal members". Marx himself said: "It is men, real living men, who do all this, who possess things and fight battles" (quoted, incongruously, by Blum himself, p. 123). We cannot, therefore, accept the new revelation: "And sociologists created societal members in their own image . . . male and female societal members created they them".[2]

(iii) The Editor goes out of his way to endorse Blum's bizarre conclusions. This endorsement can be made to throw further light on their sources. To support and explain "Blum's point" Young cites an item "of mathematicians' 'common culture'. . . .: 'It is a statistical truism that . . . half a population of kidney beans will be of shorter than average length . . . despite efforts of breeders . . . to produce longer beans . . .'." This is an inauspicious beginning. For if the word 'average' is to be interpreted in its ordinary sense, in which it is equivalent to the 'arithmetic mean' of the mathematicians, then it is not necessarily true, but plain false, that half of any population must be below average. Where one is a mere five foot and everyone else is a six-footer, there all but the first must be above the arithmetic mean height. It is the median, not the average, the arithmetic mean, which half of any population must be below.

Young continues: "the methodical character of marriages, divorces and suicides is seen and made possible by the organized practices of sociologists: likewise the inevitable normal distribution of kidney beans, the patterns of marks in examinations, and the regular 50-60% of passes in General Certificate are seen and made possible by the organized activities of breeders and examiners" (p. 10). The initial ill omens are thus fulfilled. For there is another and crucial confusion here. Suppose that the G.C.E. examinations are indeed among those in which, whether by deliberate intent, or by the workings of less conscious mechanisms in and between those in charge, the proportion of passes remains constant regardless of any annual variations in the quality of the work done. Then we do have a genuine case of a phenomenon both "seen and made possible by the organized activities of . . . examiners". It would be a gaffe to interpret the stability of the pass rate as a fact about the candidates instead of as a fact about this particular examination system. But this genuine case is as such precisely not analogous to either that of marriage, divorce and suicide or that of logically necessary truths.

It is not analogous to the former because none of the three institutions mentioned is in fact even in part an artefact of sociologists. Suppose however that the point of inserting the expression "the methodical character" is to confine the claim to what sociologists have reported as their findings in these and other areas. Suppose that the contention is that, whereas these reports pretend to inform us about "the rabble without doors", really they reveal only facts about the honoured society of the sociologists – just as the stability of the G.C.E. pass rate must be, on the assumptions stated, a fact about the examiners rather than a fact about the candidates. Then again, in so far as this is or must be so, sociology becomes a gigantic conspiracy to deceive a public which had been promised a social science. Precisely this suggestion, which is surely too offensive, is, it seems, implied by the penultimate sentence of Blum's paper: "Sociology exists because sociologists have managed to negotiate a set of practices for creating and acting upon external worlds" (p. 131).

The case of logically necessary truths is different again. The sociologist who retails some logically necessary truth as an empirical finding is not misrepresenting a fact about himself as a fact about the subjects of his research. His fault just is that of putting forward a logically necessary truth as if it were contingent. It is one thing for a student of Danish villains to find that they are all products of maternal deprivation. It is quite another for him to find that "There's ne'er a villain living in all Denmark/But he's an arrant knave". As Horatio said: "There needs no ghost, my lord, come from the grave/To tell us this" (*Hamlet,* I, v). There needs no sociologist come from Essex either.

(iv) Young refers with approval to a "discussion of how 'official statistics' on crime are produced" (p. 25). Everyone with a sophisticated interest in such matters knows that increases or declines in the numbers of reported offences in certain categories may sometimes refer to features of the system of reporting rather than to actual variations in the popularity of these offences. Thus, in the bad old pre-Wolfenden days, a sudden jump in the number of successful prosecutions for homosexual offences in – say – Bootle might have indicated, not a real explosion of unnatural vice, but the appointment of a Chief Constable with 'a thing about queers'. Young and his associates, with the overenthusiasm of the freshly initiated, are inclined without sufficient particular reason to identify this Buggery in Bootle Effect everywhere. They are especially so inclined wherever others might uninstructedly have thought that they saw evidence of real differences between pupils, or in and between subjects of instruction. This is one of the tendencies characterised as idealist in Section 1 of the present chapter.

One example, from Young himself, was examined in Subsection (iii) above. Another, more obviously and immediately relevant to current educational controversies, raises further issues. Esland writes:

> It is clear that the psychometric epistemology has been paradigmatic for much of the educational practice in Britain. . . . Not only has it had the frameworks of meaning and the criteria of truth and validity which are part of a paradigm, it also has its problems – one of which is how to get 'unintelligent' children to learn – and the methodological principles which can be legitimately employed . . . (e.g. compensatory education). This has been a massive constraint on the thinking of teachers. Their taken for granted, natural world has contained assumptions about the existence of a substance called 'intelligence', which, like 'phlogiston', is 'given off' when certain stimuli are applied to the child. If it is not manifested in certain reality defining procedures, then the child is deficient. The circularity of the epistemology thus

becomes clear. It is self-defeating and self-contradictory to assume that all children are intellectually deficient until they prove otherwise, and then to spend time and money trying to remedy what one has defined as inevitable anyway. Lacey provides an excellent illustration of the self-fulfilling nature of the teacher's definition of a 'good' pupil. The 'problem pupils' are so because of the premises on which the differentiation is made. (p. 93)

(a) Now, first, this passage with its cartoon misrepresentation of the findings of the psychometrists makes it very clear that Esland is one of those who wants to minimise, even if he cannot bring himself to deny outright, any substantial hereditarily determined and educationally relevant differences in ability, temperament or inclination. Compare Esland's position with that taken by Nell Keddie in the final paragraph of her contribution: "It seems likely that the hierarchical categories of ability and knowledge may well persist in unstreamed class-rooms and lead to the differentiation of undifferentiated curricula, because teachers differentiate in selection of content and in pedagogy between pupils perceived as of high and low ability. The origins of these categories are likely to lie outside the school and within the structure of the society itself in its wider distribution." Without apparently entertaining for one moment the thought that the perceptions of the teachers may be at least in part veridical, she concludes: "It seems likely, therefore, that innovation in schools will not be of a very radical kind unless the categories teachers use to organize what they know about pupils and to determine what counts as knowledge undergo a fundamental change" (p. 156).

Such blindness to any relevant realities which may be hereditarily determined is an occupational temptation for sociologists. For whatever is not socially determined is not open to sociological explanation; and sociologists, like other people, are prone to jurisdictional imperialism. About this there will be more later, in Chapter 4.

(b) Second, the circularity and self-contradiction so triumph-antly proclaimed by Esland are not there. To say hypothetically that if intelligence "is not manifested . . . then the child is deficient", is not categorically to maintain that "all children are intellectually deficient". To offer a programme of "compensatory education" in response to a deficiency which supposedly cannot be helped is not to contradict yourself, by proposing to alter what you yourself have said to be inevitable and unalterable. Nor is to assume or, better, to presume "that all children are intellectually deficient until they prove otherwise", to assume that they all are thus deficient, period; any more than to presume that all defendants are innocent until and unless they are proved guilty, is to assume that all defendants are innocent, period. The general presumption of innocence is concerned with where the public burden of proof must lie, not with what we may happen privately to believe or even to know in any particular case. (See, for instance, Flew: 6, 1.)

This distinction between a categorical assumption and a defeasible presumption is also needed in Nell Keddie's paper. She gives some shocking examples of bad teaching, in which teachers put children down for asking what were in fact pointed and pertinent questions (pp. 140, 153, and 158 n.35): I myself warmed especially to the first of these three questioners, who was so – shall we say? – reactionary as to want to learn some geography rather than to be subjected to "socialization". These and other examples Keddie interprets in terms of her theory "that C stream pupils disrupt teachers' expectations and violate their norms of appropriate social, moral and intellectual pupil behaviour" (p. 134); and, in particular, that "teachers tend not to perceive the collective social class basis of pupils' experience" (p. 142). Keddie also contrives to mention one alleged mixture of sensitivity with inhibition which I find blankly unbelievable: "Frequently C, and occasionally B pupils become 'characters'; for example 'Clare will envelop Dick one of these days. The girls think Dick is very sexy'. *A stream pupils are not spoken of in this way*" (p. 143: italics supplied).

But, however much or however little truth there may be in all this, we must also point a moral quite independent of social class. The fact that a group of children has been by I.Q. tests or otherwise more or less efficiently selected for dullness, or for cleverness, provides no sufficient warrant for assuming that no child in that group will ever do or say anything clever, or stupid, as the case may be. We are dealing here only with averages and with what is generally so. Such premises can at most justify defeasible presumptions. Children who on average, or generally, are dull can nevertheless be expected to produce occasional flashes; and any teacher worthy of the name ought to be ever ready to notice, to welcome and to exploit those flashes. We shall be returning to this simple but important logical point in Chapter 5, considering it then in the highly explosive context of race.

(c) The third point against Esland requires a distinction between two senses of 'make' and other usually causal words. It is a distinction familiar to critical students of Plato's Theory of Forms. Consider the question: 'What makes living things alive?' This may be interpreted in two totally different ways. In one it is asking what constitutes life, what is the meaning of the word 'life'. In the other it is asking what produces the phenomena so labelled. We can pick out the first 'makes' as 'makes' (constitutive) and the second as 'makes' (causal). It now becomes obvious that it would be absurd to maintain that the criteria of life – the principles, that is, upon which we distinguish living things from non-living – produce the actual living things by making (causal) alive what was not alive before. (For a fuller account of this distinction, and for an exposition of the theory itself, see Flew: 4, II, IV, especially IV, § 4.

Esland concludes: "The 'problem pupils' are so because of the premises on which the differentiation is made"; and he clearly thinks that he has demonstrated that to solve the problem of such problem pupils it is necessary and sufficient to change the offending criteria – "the premises on which the differentiation is made". For he goes on in his next sentence: "Some teachers, unwilling to accept this inexorable logic, seek to legitimate their definitions by reference to the social conditions, which, by being thought capable of retarding or promoting learning, can be held 'responsible' for educational problems . . ." (p. 93).[3]

(d) Fourth, this grotesque confusion, so proudly paraded as a trophy of "inexorable logic", is supported and intensified by an appeal to empirical research: "Lacey provides an excellent illustration of the self-fulfilling nature of the teacher's definition of a 'good' pupil" (p. 93). This is a reference to an article on 'Some Sociological Concomitants of Academic Streaming' in the *British Journal of Sociology*, vol. XVII, no. 3 (1966). This article seems to me in fact to do little, if anything, to show what Esland says that it shows. Nevertheless there is something genuine and educationally important here, something of which we have to take full account. Pupils, and not pupils only, often strive to fulfil the expectations which others have of them. Let us, in tribute to Lord Nelson, call this the England Expects Effect.

It must be distinguished from the Buggery in Bootle Effect described at the beginning of the present Subsection (iv). For, whereas that makes it seem that there has been some actual change in what we are investigating, when really we have no good reason to believe that this is so, in this real changes are made by the awareness of the expectations. But, just as it is wrong to assume without particular reasons that all evidence for objective human differences can be explained away by reference to the former, so it is equally wrong to assume that all the actual observed differences have been produced by different expectations. Such expectations themselves may be, and often are, grounded in knowledge of antecedent talents and temperament. Nor are we all, even within the limits of our various talents, the creatures of other people's expectations. Some of us are more or less indifferent, while with others such recognised expectations may be counter-productive. Nor is it always the least admirable pupil, or person, who responds by saying through clenched teeth: 'So that's what they think about me. I'll show them!'.[4]

3.   *The Theory of Knowledge of Sociologico-criticism*

We saw in Section 1 that the main aim of *Knowledge and Control* is to put the sociology of knowledge in the centre of the sociology of education. Whereas, the Editor says, in the past "Sociologists, in this country and in the USA, have hardly considered the *content* of education" (p. 10: his emphasis), in this book "sociology of education is no longer conceived as an area of enquiry distinct from the sociology of knowledge" (p. 3). Certainly – as Ioan Davies of the Queen's University, Ontario, says in the final paper – "what is often taken to be the sociology of education is not primarily about education at all – but about selection and stratification, socialization and organizations" (p. 273). You can, and will need to, say that again.

For much the same is true of what are proposed today as educational reforms by many professional administrators and educationalists also. Consider, as one telltale instance, the Foreword written by Tyrrell Burgess for the British edition of an outstanding recent contribution to educational sociology, *Inequality*. Burgess commends the authors for "stating the liberal and radical assumptions about education and then testing them against the evidence". To Burgess "The conclusion seems inescapable: reforming the schools will not bring about social change. . . ." He goes on: "To almost any proposal for education we can now ask 'did it survive the Jencks test?'. And, if not, we can further ask 'What explicit steps are proposed to fend off failure this time?'. . . . A clue to the way we ought to do this can be found in the experience of the schools. Their failure as engines of social change. . . ." (Jencks, pp. 1 and 2). For the educationalist Burgess, as for so many other educationalists today, a policy for education or an educational policy is a policy for egalitarian social engineering; and an educational failure is by no means necessarily a failure in learning or teaching.

If Young's proposal for an intellectual revolution raises the spirits of anyone still so old-fashioned as to believe that education is, or should be, centrally concerned with the acquisition of various kinds of knowledge; then they are, I am afraid, in for a quick disappointment. For Young, as for most of his colleagues, to "explore the implications of treating knowledge, or 'what counts as knowledge', as socially constituted or constructed" (p. 5) necessarily involves "the subversion of absolutism by sociology" (p. 6). This in turn is apparently taken to imply that the differences between disciplines, and even knowledge itself, are all illusions, destined to be shattered by the revolutionary advance of sociology.

(i) "Much research in education", Young says, "starts from an absolutist view of cognitive categories such as 'rational' and 'abstract'. This view in effect prevents these categories from being treated as themselves socially constructed and therefore open to sociological enquiry" (p. 11). If the word 'absolute' is to be construed thus, as precluding sociological inquiry, then the absolutist is indeed exposed as an obscurantist. Whatever the merits or demerits of these or any other concepts, it should be obvious that there is room for questions about how we in fact come to have and to use those concepts which we do have and use.

But a little later we find Young objecting generally to the work of the philosophers of education – Paul Hirst in particular: "The problem with this kind of critique is that it appears to be based on an absolutist conception of a set of distinct forms of knowledge which correspond closely to the traditional areas of the academic curriculum and thus justify, rather than examine, what are no more than the socio-historical constructs of a particular time. It is important to stress that it is . . . forms of understanding that it is claimed are 'necessarily' distinct. The point I wish to make here is that unless such *necessary* distinctions or intrinsic logics are treated as problematic, philosophical criticism cannot examine the assumptions of academic curricula" (p. 23: Young's italics).

The word 'absolutist' is here no longer employed in the original sense. For Hirst is being faulted: not for obstructing sociological investigation of how we come to make the distinctions; but for concluding that the distinctions made do in fact refer to actual differences. Not having noticed this crucial shift in meaning, Young has omitted to offer any reason for his own confident insistence: that the various concepts under discussion "are no more than the socio-historical constructs of a particular time"; and hence, presumably, that they do not correspond to any actual, perhaps necessary and universal, differences. It is one thing to say that certain notions are "the socio-historical constructs of a particular time". It is quite another to add that they are *no more than* "the socio-historical constructs of a particular time". The move from a statement of the first, straight to a conclusion of the second sort – without further reason given – is as illegitimate as it is common. It cannot be right to proceed from a premise stating only that this is that direct to the richer conclusion that this is *merely* that, that this is *nothing but* that, that this is that *and nothing else*. Let us, therefore, introduce the appropriately shaming nickname 'The Debunker's Fallacy'. (See my *'Merely* and *Nothing But'* in *The Listener,* 1 October 1964; and compare Flew: 7, passim.)

If only Young had formulated his final contention a little more carefully, it could have been unexceptionable. For it must be necessarily true to say that unless supposedly essential distinctions and allegedly intrinsic logics are treated as problematic, philosophical criticism cannot examine the assumptions of academic curricula. But then we have to notice that nothing has been said to show that Hirst failed to satisfy this requirement. It was, surely, precisely the problem of what, if any, differences are essential, and intrinsic, and a matter of logic, which Hirst set himself to solve. (See Hirst, passim.) The reason why Young fails to see this is that he shares the too-common assumption that it is a necessary, indeed perhaps the sufficient, condition of a critical approach that such an approach must result in the rejection of some established belief. That this is, though popular, a misconception of the nature of criticism is manifest when we ask whether the only genuine Shakespearean critics are those who can bring themselves to think that Shakespeare is, after all, no good.

(ii) The central mistake exposed in the previous Subsection (i) is that of assuming that sociological investigation must always reveal – even perhaps presuppose – that there are no actual differences reflected by any distinctions which it can 'treat as problematic'. Slightly more complicated versions of the same disastrous mistake are found in treatments of the stratification of knowledge. Just as Young is never prepared to allow that sociological investigation could fail to unmask existing assumptions and evaluations as without foundation: so it never enters his head that some courses might not merely be thought to be, but actually be, more demanding than others – and that this might be at least one of the bases on which they are in fact accorded either high or low status.

Certainly subjects are not just difficult in themselves. What you or I find difficult or easy depends in part both on what training we have had and on our natural endowments. But none of this is any reason for denying, what is in fact true, that there are also differences between subjects as well as between students. I will not here resist the temptation to quote the arch-élitist Plato. For, in winding up the case for mathematics as the perfect propædeutic for the peculiar education of Guardians, *The Republic* says: " – And, furthermore, my conviction is that we shall not easily find disciplines which are harder work for the student and for the practitioner, nor many of them' – 'That's for sure' – 'Then for all these reasons, we must not neglect that study, but those with the best natural endowments must be so educated' – 'I agree', he said" (§ 526C).

Both the two varieties of doctrinally motivated scotoma distinguished in the previous paragraph are displayed in Young's comment on some recent Schools Council innovations: "Firstly, by taking the assumptions of the academic curricula for granted, the social evaluations of knowledge implicit in such curricula are by implication being assumed to be in some sense 'absolute' and therefore not open to enquiry. Secondly, by creating new courses in 'low status' knowledge areas, and restricting their availability to those who have already failed in terms of academic definitions of knowledge, these failures are seen as individual failures, either of motivation, ability or circumstances, and not failures of the academic system itself" (p. 40).

Again, in considering "the unquestioned dimensions of academic curricula" it is obvious to Young that "these characteristics can be seen as social definitions of educational value, and thus become problematic in the sense that if they persist it is not because knowledge is in any meaningful way best made available according to the criteria they represent, but because they are conscious or unconscious cultural choices which accord with the values and beliefs of dominant groups at a particular time" (p. 38). Of course, "these characteristics can be seen as social definitions of educational value". In this aspect we can raise the questions how in fact this society came to have these values; and what desires and interests are involved in maintaining – or, for that matter, in challenging – such established commitments. But then, again of course, these possibilities are not sufficient to show that knowledge is not "best made available according to the criteria they represent". Whether or not it is, is another and separate question.

Young's mistake can in turn be seen as one more example of a familiar fatal movement. The cobbler begins by admitting, 'I am professionally concerned and qualified to deal only with leather'. He goes on to say, more enthusiastically, 'Nothing like leather'. He ends by holding, triumphantly, 'Nothing but leather'. A modest confession of professional limitation is thus transformed into a piece of reckless deflationary metaphysics.

Compare a parallel statement by a leading English Freudian: "To achieve success the analyst must above all be an analyst. That is to say, he must know positively that all human emotional reactions, all human judgements and even reason itself, are but the tools of the unconscious; that such seemingly acute convictions which an intelligent person like this possesses are but the inevitable effect of causes which lie buried in the unconscious levels of his psyche" (Berg, p. 190). Certainly Berg is entitled to insist that the analyst in his therapeutic hours should consider only the conscious or unconscious motives of the utterances of his patients. But it is a different thing entirely to go on to suggest that neither these nor any other utterances constitute true judgements or good reasons. Not merely does this wholesale and universal conclusion not follow from the initial, limited, professional manifesto. It also and necessarily undermines the analyst's pretensions to possess any rational warrant for his own theory and practice.[5]

(iii) Whatever may be true of sociology in general, the sociology of knowledge cannot abstract completely from at least one kind of value-commitment. Even where neutrality is possible with regard to the cognitive status of the beliefs to which this study refers, there still has to be some involvement with standards of evidence and logic if any belief is to be identified as the belief it is.

For simplicity's sake ignore all linguistic possibilities but those of English. To establish that someone believes that there is gold in them thar hills it is not sufficient to observe that he has with apparent conviction uttered the words: 'There is gold in them thar hills'. It is also necessary to establish some modicum of rational aptness in his responses to claims which are either entailed by or incompatible with, or which constitute evidence either for or against, the claim in question. 'Belief', that is to say, is not a purely psychological word: it is in part a term of logical appraisal.

Furthermore, there are at least some questions proper to the sociology of knowledge which themselves presuppose a commitment to the correctness or incorrectness of certain of the beliefs to which they refer. Young mentions a study in which tests in applied mathematics were given to two groups: one of primitive Kpelle people; and the other of U.S. Peace Corps volunteers. The (not very hard) problem is to explain why the former did so much better than the latter on questions about the number of cups of rice that could be obtained from a large bowl, whereas the standings were reversed on questions which involved sorting cards. Young comments: "to describe the Kpelle performance in the second test as evidence of limited mathematical ability is no more justified than to describe the American volunteers' errors in the first test as inept, unless we already start with preconceptions of mathematical competence" (p. 12).

Certainly it would be wrong to accept the performance of either group in either test as adequate proof of either general mathematical talent or the lack of it. Equally certainly the conduct and interpretation of any such tests presuppose standards of correct and incorrect performance; and, in so far as the tests are mathematical, standards of correct and incorrect in mathematics. It is precisely for this second reason that the moral drawn by Young is diametrically wrong: "The general point, therefore, is that if we do not begin by assuming what mathematical (or other) knowledge is, we can compare the way, under different social and economic conditions, men have conducted different styles of thought and kinds of explanation" (p. 12).

On the contrary: if we are not permitted to recognise that there is a correct or incorrect in mathematics, a true or false in statements about the world, a right or wrong in explanation; then we are not permitted to see what our subjects thought they were doing under their "different social and economic conditions"; and we cannot even begin to explain to our Kpelle and Peace Corps volunteers what it is that we want them to do. Young, like several of his fellow contributors, is much impressed by Thomas Kuhn's *The Structure of Scientific Revolutions.* I shall have rather more to say about that book in Chapter 3. But I must repeat here at once one most fundamental objection put by Paul Feyerabend: "Kuhn, as we interpret him now and as he himself very often wants to be interpreted, has failed to do one important thing. He has failed to discuss the *aim* of science" (Lakatos and Musgrave, p. 201: italics original).

(iv) No doubt it is often possible for sociology to remain neutral about the cognitive status of particular beliefs or even about the claims of particular disciplines. But our next job is to notice another way in which what starts as an attempt at neutrality with regard to such a claim may slide into its more or less contemptuous rejection. This slide may be compared especially with that already noticed in Subsection (ii), by which a statement of professional limitation is transformed into a piece of deflationary metaphysics. The basic trouble here is that all the usual devices by which we may try to detach ourselves from the cognitive commitments of others are also devices for expressing one sort or another of disfavour towards those commitments. If we speak of someone's putative, supposed, alleged or assumed knowledge, then this is almost bound to suggest that we have some positive ground for doubting their claim to know. If we put the word 'knowledge' between inverted commas, then these are likely to be read as sneer quotes.

These dangers are in *Knowledge and Control* often compounded by simple carelessness. Thus Young complains that within one "framework the content of education is taken as a 'given' . . . the 'educational failures' become a sort of 'deviant' " (p. 25). The first and the third of these three sets of inverted commas are out of place. For, although he certainly does not want to commit himself to saying that those who are in this context called educational failures really are, part of his reason for reluctance is that within this disfavoured framework the content of education is – but, he thinks, wrongly – taken as given. Nor does he really want to deny that these alleged – but perhaps not actual – educational failures are truly deviants from the no doubt misbegotten norms of that bad old framework.

Again, Young writes that "teachers who for years have successfully produced good 'A' level results from highly selected groups of pupils are now faced with many pupils who appear neither to know how to 'learn' the 'academic knowledge', nor appear to want to" (pp. 21-2). Since the inverted commas within this quotation can scarcely be construed as marking non-committal or non-standard employments, I can only suggest that they are intended to express a strong distaste both for learning and for academic knowledge. (Students of the theoretical writings of J. V. Stalin will recall how often the word 'liberalism' is escorted by inverted commas: not because it is being mentioned rather than used; nor because Stalin wishes to reproach 'liberalism' for not being truly liberalism; but precisely and only because real liberalism is something which, like any Leninist, he hates.[6]) Young's comment upon his own sentence just quoted is wholly characteristic: "This inevitably poses for teachers quite new problems of finding alternatives" (p. 22).[7] It is to my mind curious that those who have no good to say of the market mechanism in its proper place, nor of capitalism, should so often be willing to insist that in education the (reluctant) customer is always right.[8]

(v) Another temptation to conclude that the sociology of knowledge must always assume or reveal that the beliefs to which it refers are unfounded, lies in the fact that in everyday non-scientific contexts we usually ask for or provide psychological or sociological explanations for the making of assertions only when the content of those assertions is thought to be legitimately suspect. (The temptation, to which people are yielding all the time, is to mistake the truth or even the mere possibility of such an explanation for a demonstration that any suspicions would be abundantly justified.)

Suppose, for example, we discover that so celebrated a literary guru as Raymond Williams makes elementary mistakes in his Modern Masters study of *George Orwell*. For instance, Williams does in fact maintain that what he lists as the Newspeak word 'speedwise' is now "ominously familiar". But that word does not in fact appear in *1984*, and belongs rather to the journalistic telegraphese of Evelyn Waugh's *Scoop*. Again, Williams commends Orwell as "an intransigent enemy of every kind of *thoughtcrime*" (Williams, p. 75, Orwell's italics). The word 'thoughtcrime' was coined in *1984*. But it is used to characterise, while simultaneously execrating, only heretical deviations from the norms of Ingsoc party doctrine. Orwell was on the side of the victims, not the persecutors; for the heretics, and against Ingsoc.

Puzzled by such unscholarly lapses in so highly regarded a critic, we seek some explanation. Perhaps we recall *May Day Manifesto 1968*, and conjecture that its editor is scarcely likely to have been writing with a cherished and recently re-read copy of *1984* open on his desk. For so extreme and authoritarian a socialist Orwell's last appalling nightmare of totalitarianism must be an embarrassment – indeed an exercise in thoughtcrime!

Such explanations never are, though they are much too often mistaken to be, proper substitutes for proofs that the lapses to be explained really are lapses – and not in fact perfectly true expressions, or otherwise correct. So, that the layman usually seeks them only where he is already persuaded that the content of the belief, or whatever else, is with reason cognitively, or otherwise, suspect, could not by itself justify the conclusion that suspicions here must be well founded. The sociologist of knowledge is, however, professionally committed to pressing his questions even where there is no reason at all to think that there is anything wrong. In whatever other ways his studies may have to be value-free or value-loaded, he must in his working hours be as much concerned with the social background and the social preconditions of an educational set up in which the known truth or the best evidenced guesses are presented as near as may be straight, as he will be with those of others where indeed "All knowledge is shrouded in ideology" (M. F. D. Young, p. 282).

4. *How the Sociologists Blum and Esland Deny Objectivity*

The very fact that the scope of the sociology of knowledge thus extends beyond the normal interests of the layman is, therefore, the reason why it is doubly wrong for spokesmen for the ambitions of that discipline to assume that the possibility of a sociological explanation of the emergence and popularity of a belief must be in itself sufficient refutation of its content. But these present spokesmen have in any case little time for any notion of straight knowledge of truths altogether independent of the knower. Young, for instance, faults "an otherwise excellent paper" by Rytina and Loomis in a most characteristic fashion: "After criticizing Marx and Dewey for using *metaphysical* justifications of the truth of what men 'know' in terms of what men 'do', they do likewise in drawing on a *metaphysical* 'out there' in terms of which, they claim, we must check out our theories against our practice" (p. 43, his italics).

(i) Similarly idealist notions are sketched a little more fully by both Esland and Blum. The latter states: "Scholars who have traditionally sought to discover 'objective' knowledge have had to contend with the fact that the search for and discovery of such knowledge is socially organized. ... The implication is this: if objective knowledge is taken to mean knowledge of a reality independent of language, or presuppositionless knowledge, or knowledge of the world which is independent of the observer's procedures for finding and producing the knowledge, then there is no such thing as objective knowledge" (p. 128).

(a) If only Blum had spelt out his points with a few elementary illustrations it would have been easier for everyone – and not least Blum – to discern what this particular denial of objective knowledge amounts to. First, if he really means to deny "knowledge of a reality independent of language", then his denial is ridiculous. It is ridiculous to maintain, for instance, that the stars in their courses are in any way dependent on what we say or do not say; and it is not for any sociologist to deny the claims of the natural scientists to know that this earth existed long before it bore any language-using creatures: "Natural science positively asserts that the earth once existed in such a state that no man or any other creature existed or could have existed on it" (Lenin, p. 69).

If instead Blum really means to deny only propositional knowledge independent of language, then this is unexceptionable. Or, rather, it is unexceptionable so long as it is not mistaken to imply that the truths which we have to express in a particular form of words would not be true at all until and unless someone had formulated those truths in these or equivalent words. The crucial distinctions are: first, between knowing, and the truths which are known; and, second, between knowledge of a reality which is independent of language, and knowledge which is itself independent of language. It is one thing, and scarcely disputatious, to say that the extent of our knowledge must be limited by, among other things, the quality and the quantity of the conceptual equipment which happens to be available to us. It is quite another and, as Lenin has just reminded us, utterly paradoxical and preposterous to say that any reality of which we can have knowledge must be in part dependent upon us and our concepts.

(b) Second, the same distinctions need to be applied in considering Blum's denial of any "knowledge of the world which is independent of the observer's procedures". If Blum wants us to construe this as involving that we do not know that there is a world which is independent of our observation, which preceded, and which will outlast it, then this is again metaphysical idealism, untrue, and by all of us known to be untrue. (In Chapter 3 I shall go on to suggest that, besides being incompatible with innumerable known facts, such idealism cannot even be communicated without presupposing its own falsity.) If on the other hand all that Blum really wanted to assert was that no one can know anything without knowing it, or that anyone's claim to know anything must ultimately be grounded in their own experience, then these claims too would be unexceptionable.

Yet, having said this, it becomes necessary for future reference to distinguish two fundamentally different senses of 'experience'. In the primary – let us call it the public sense – to say that she has had experience of computers is to say that she has been in contact with a certain sort of objects 'without the mind'. In the secondary and more sophisticated sense – let us call it private – to say that he has enjoyed a certain kind of experience is not necessarily to say that he has had any contact with anything 'without the mind'. The man who 'sees' hallucinatory rabbits precisely does not see any actual rabbits: his experience of rabbits is, therefore, experience of rabbits only in the second but not in the first sense. If the empiricist claim that anyone's claim to know anything must ultimately be grounded in their own experience is interpreted as referring to public experience, then it is essentially materialist. But if it is instead to be interpreted as referring to private experience, then – as the whole story of philosophy since Descartes shows very clearly – the empiricist has his feet on a downhill road to idealism and solipsism. Obviously it is only in the former interpretation of the second reading of Blum's remarks about "the observer's procedures" that I have just passed what he might have said as innocuous.

(ii) Esland makes an unpromising start: "Due to the wide methodological acceptance among sociologists of what has been called an anti-humanistic scientism, there has been a readiness to leave epistemological issues to philosophy, on the assumption that 'knowing' derives from what is verifiable" (p. 70). We are offered no reason why it should be thought that the territory of philosophical epistemology ought to be annexed by sociology. Nor are we told why it is, apparently, wrong to assume that questions about knowledge must be very closely connected with questions about truth, verification and verifiability. It is not a strong testimonial for Esland as an aspiring epistemologist that he does not, apparently, recognise that to know a proposition is to know that that proposition is true; and hence that there is a logically necessary connection between knowledge and truth.

He is more forthcoming, but no better, when he proceeds to denounce "the objectivistic view of knowledge . . . the view represented in traditional epistemology and analytic philosophy". Objectivism in this sense "has been firmly embedded in the norms and rituals of academic culture and its transmission"; and it is also, he admits, "how knowledge is conceived in the reality of everyday experience where the taken for granted nature of the world is rarely questioned. The individual consciousness recognizes objects as being 'out there', as coercive, external realities" (p. 75).

So what? What is wrong with that? Well, it seems that such

objectivism is the ultimate source of all things which any Penguin Educationalist holds bad: "Objectivity meant the transcending of socio-cultural influences and validation by universal reason. ... Objectivism became very much an optimistic ethic for progressivism and liberalism, and a rationale for the maintenance of political élitism and the gradualness of political emancipation in Britain ... the teacher was, and still is, exhorted to develop the 'rationality' of the learner. ... The simplistic notion of 'progressivism' has been preserved in the belief in scientific neutralism, value-freedom, and 'liberal education' " (p. 76). And so on.

To such objectivism Esland's objection, deriving he says ultimately from Hegel and the young Marx, is that it represents man "not as world-producer but as world-produced. We have, therefore, a reified philosophy in which objectivity is auton-omized and which does not regard as problematical for the constituency of the object its constitution in the subjective experience of individuals. One finds it difficult to disagree with the claim that this epistemology is fundamentally dehumaniz-ing" (p. 75).

Wait a minute. Refuse to be browbeaten. Certainly it is difficult to know where to begin to disagree with someone who appeals to the authority of Marx as a metaphysical idealist: was it not the young Marx who began by standing Hegel on his head; or, rather, by re-establishing Hegel's system on materialist foundations putting it the right way up? Do not be put off by Esland's constipated misemployment of the word 'constituency' where the sense requires 'constitution'. His rejection of ob-jectivism, where this rejection requires that the constitution of the (public) object must be in some way dependent on our (private) thoughts about it ("its [constitution] in the subjective experience of individuals"), is, once again, and despite the incongruous genuflexion towards Marx as well as Hegel, metaphysical idealism. And, although Esland "finds it difficult to disagree with the claim" that any objectivist or – in Marxist terms – materialist epistemology is "fundamentally dehumaniz-ing", this is from him nothing but bluster and bullying. No reason or explanation is given. We are left to conjecture that, since the Eslandian idealist holds that it is of the essence of man to be – like the theist God – "world-producer" not "world-produced", therefore for Esland any recognition of the actual and somewhat humbler human condition must be "fundamentally dehumanizing".

He continues, citing the same articles by Wright Mills to which back in Section 1 we noticed Young referring: "It should be emphasized that questions of 'truth' and 'validity' are also problematic. . . . 'There have been, and are diverse canons . . . themselves, in their persistence and change, open to socio-historical relativization' . . . the cognitive tradition which forms an epistemology can exist only through a supporting community of people. Its members are co-producers of reality and the survival of this reality depends on its continuing plausibility to the community" (pp. 77-8: sneer quotes, and the lack of them, original).

It follows, therefore, that all issues of truth, validity and reality depend – like the existence of Tinker Bell in the pantomime – upon what some community brings itself to believe. Pierre Bourdieu, who is not himself infected by this total relativism, quotes a relevant passage from the psychologist Kurt Lewin: "Experiments dealing with memory and group pressure on the individual show that what exists as 'reality' for the individual is, to a high degree, determined by what is socially accepted as reality. . . . 'Reality' therefore, is not an absolute. It differs with the group to which the individual belongs" (p. 195). This is both true and important. But it is true only when read correctly. What Lewin is saying is: not that reality is not an absolute, because it differs with the group to which the individual belongs; but that 'reality' – that is to say what someone believes about reality – is not an absolute, because it varies a lot with the group to which that individual belongs.

Interactions between reality and 'reality' – "dialectical" interactions, if Esland insists (p. 77) – are of central importance in human affairs; and hence for historiography, sociology and all the other human sciences too. We act on the world and on other people guided or misguided by what we believe about it, and them; while it, and they, affect us and our beliefs about it, and them.

Consider, for instance, what the military historian needs in order fully to understand the battle. It is not sufficient, although it is absolutely necessary, that he should know where all the forces were, and when, and what movements occurred, and with what results; and all these forces, and movements, and results are, of course, forces and movements and results 'without the mind'. It is also necessary for him to know what the participants believed and what they wanted, and how these beliefs and desires were related both to the decisions which they made, and to the facts as they actually were 'without the minds' of those making these decisions. That the panzer commander led his spearhead straight into an ambush of anti-tank guns and mines becomes intelligible only in terms of an account of the relation, or lack of relation, between his beliefs about his situation and his actual situation.

It is, therefore, egregiously wrongheaded – in the name, of all things, of the sociology of knowledge – to deny the reality and knowability of any independent reality; and hence to deny the possibility of this distinction between his 'reality' and the realities. The sociologico-criticism of *Knowledge and Control* first identifies the sociology of education with the sociology of knowledge, and then presents the latter as necessarily revealing that all the educationally relevant differences between pupils and in and between subjects of study are nothing but the shadows cast by conflicting social forces. This is enough to make the new sociology of education an anti-educational activity. But the idealist revelation, which this sociologico-criticism mistakes to be the outcome and main content of sociological enlightenment, is also, and even more fundamentally, incompatible with basic presuppositions both of science in general and of the social sciences in particular. In Esland the offence is exacerbated by his accusing all those not subject to this extraordinary group negative hallucination of involvement in a conspiracy to dehumanise.

3 Reality, Rationality, and the Possibility of Anthropology

One paper in *Knowledge and Control* is in quite a different class from all the others. This is Robin Horton's 'African Traditional Thought and Western Science'. But its main appeal to Young is its one serious weakness. Young says: "Formal education is based on the assumption that thought systems organized in curricula are in some sense 'superior' to the thought systems of those who are to be (or have not been) educated. It is just this implicit 'superiority' that Horton is questioning when he compares Western and African 'theoretical' thought in his paper" (p. 13).

Certainly Young is right about the assumption: all educational activity does indeed take it for granted that, all other things being equal, it is better to be educated than to be uneducated, and better to be well educated than to be badly educated. If and in so far as either Young himself or any of his associates cannot accept this, then they ought to face the question of the propriety of their remaining as teachers in Departments and Institutes of Education; or indeed of their holding positions anywhere else in what Dr Tom Lehrer so lightly labels Edbiz. But I shall not refer again to this existential challenge. Instead the present chapter will be devoted to the examination, and the removal, of some of the supports most commonly offered for the educationally and scientifically disastrous conclusion that there is here neither superiority nor inferiority. The aim is to subvert the popular subversive doctrine proclaimed – apparently without embarrassment – by Donald Swift, Professor of Education in the Open University: "And, finally, we cannot accept quality distinctions between cultures" (Richardson and Spears, p. 156).

1. *In What Way Does Robin Horton Repudiate Idealism and Superstition?*

Horton begins by distinguishing two predicaments, one closed and the other open. "The first possibility is simply a continuance of the magical world-view. If ideas and words are inextricably bound up with reality, and if indeed they shape it and control it, then a multiplicity of idea-systems means a multiplicity of realities, and a change of ideas means a change of things. But whereas there is nothing particularly absurd or inconsistent about this view it is clearly intolerable. . . . For it means that the world is in the last analysis dependent on human whim . . . that human beings can expect to find no sort of anchor in reality" (p. 235).

He assimilates philosophical idealism to this closed predicament. Certainly that "does not say that words create, sustain and have power over that which they represent. Rather, it says that material things are 'in the mind'. That is, the mind creates, sustains and has power over matter." But this difference, Horton suggests, still leaves such idealism "little more than a post-Cartesian transposition" of the old closed predicament (p. 235).

Certainly there are contexts where we should need to underline differences; just as there are others which would require some development of distinctions within idealism itself. Like behaviourism, for instance, idealism may be either metaphysical or analytical or methodological. Where the metaphysical behaviourist holds that there is, ultimately, no such phenomenon as consciousness; the metaphysical idealist holds that everything is, again ultimately, either mind or mind-dependent. Where the analytical behaviourist maintains that mental words and expressions can be wholly analysed in terms of the actual or possible behaviour of the organism; the analytical idealist maintains that all talk about material things is similarly reducible to talk about actual or possible private perceptual experience; he is more usually called, simply, a phenomenalist. The methodological behaviourist does not as such deny consciousness. Instead he asserts that it is not possible, or at any rate not profitable, to study anything but behaviour. His idealist opposite number eschews any outright denial of existence 'without the mind', or any assertion that such talk must be senseless. Instead he says, while perhaps even asserting the bare existence of 'things-in-themselves', that all we can ever know is our own experience (presumably private). Unlike that splendid, albeit outrageous, consistent idealist Berkeley, he is one of those, including both Hume and Kant, whom Lenin, following Engels, rates and berates as "agnostics" (Lenin, pp. 13-31).

However, having allowed that there are differences of which on another occasion we should need to take account, we can now take note that Horton's "magical world-view" is as similar to the sociologico-idealism of several of his fellow contributors as that in turn is to any traditional idealism. But, whereas they are infatuated by their "magical world-view", and endorse it as the new sociological revelation, Horton is appalled. He turns for refuge to his "second possibility" which promises "an escape from this horrific prospect. It is based on the faith that while ideas and words change, there must be some anchor, some constant reality. This faith leads to the modern view of words and reality as independent variables. ... Intellectually, this second possibility is neither more nor less respectable than the first" (p. 235).

(i) To make out his thesis that the two predicaments are intellectually on all fours Horton affirms that attempts to refute idealism are "invariably, a farce". He refers to G. E. Moore. This reference is not to 'The Refutation of Idealism' in the *Philosophical Studies,* but to 'A Defence of Common Sense' in J. H. Muirhead (ed.), *Contemporary British Philosophy.* Horton dismisses Moore's characteristic appeal to familiar fact as "A gesture of faith rather than of reason, if ever there was one. . . . Smug rationalists who congratulate themselves on their freedom from magical thinking would do well to reflect on the nature of this freedom!" (p. 236).

This is altogether wrong. There can be no more rational, relevant, and decisive refutation of a universal proposition than a falsifying counter-example. If someone puts it to us that time is unreal, then there is no better nor quicker way of proving that what he has said is false than to cite some simple temporal fact: 'After breakfast I started to revise my lecture notes'. Or suppose someone tells us that "it is not an objectively discernible purely existing external world which accounts for sociology; it is the methods and procedures of sociology which create and sustain that world" (p. 131). Then the truth value of this contention is most swiftly demonstrated by referring to one or two not always very ancient peoples who contrived somehow to conduct more or less satisfactory social lives in places and periods in which no one had ever heard of sociologists.

Of course, the philosopher confronted by a philosophical paradox must go much further than this. Above all he has to come to grips with the arguments behind the paradox. But to say that refutation is not sufficient is not to say that it is not a sufficient refutation. Horton never, it seems, gets around to explaining why in his view such refutation is not refutation at all. I suspect that the reason is that he, along with so many of our contemporaries, confuses persuasion with proof: a refutation is dismissed as not really a refutation because it would not in fact carry universal conviction; and, in particular, because the idealist himself would most likely not accept it as such.

This debilitating confusion is both expressed in and encouraged by many currently common practices. People say that you cannot *prove* this or that *to* so and so; without deciding whether they are complaining of the impossibility of *proving* this or that; or of the impossibility of *persuading* so and so – the so and so! People – especially interviewers labouring to maintain a proper neutrality – say: 'But somebody or other would not agree'. They ask: 'Who is to decide?' Yet the former is no objection at all; until and unless, that is, some supporting reason is added to the bald statement of disagreement. Nor is the utterance of the interrogative by itself sufficient to establish, either that the balance between the rival arguments is as near as makes no matter even, or that there is in this particular case no question of any objective truth or falsehood. The right response to the statement that someone disagrees is, therefore, usually: either, 'On what grounds?'; or, 'So what?'. To the rhetorical question, 'Who is to decide?' it is, similarly, a no-nonsense and no-shirking, 'Us; and so let's get on with it'.

(ii) Horton asserts that "there is nothing particularly absurd or inconsistent" about "the magical world-view", and hence about idealism. We saw in Chapter 2 that, in so far as any contingent proposition can be absurd, some of the implications of idealism are absurd. It may nevertheless be more persuasive, as well as of greater philosophical interest, to outline an argument to the conclusion that any non-solipsistic idealism must be inconsistent. This argument will in the end be better appreciated if we approach rather indirectly.

(a) Lenin's *Materialism and Empirio-Criticism* has two great merits, which together make it a most remarkable achievement for a philosophical amateur writing in 1908. First, the author had as a heresy hunter an infallible nose for the idealist presuppositions and idealist implications of positions which their own proposers often had not seen to be thus infected. To avoid retreading exactly the same ground, consider the concluding words of *The Foundations of Empirical Knowledge*, a classic of Logical Positivism first published in 1940: "The most that we can do is to elaborate a technique for predicting the course of our sensory experience, and to adhere to it so long as it is found to be reliable. And this is all that is essentially involved in our belief in the reality of the physical world" (Ayer: 2, p. 274).

It is clear enough – and this interpretation is supported by everything which goes before – that the word 'experience' here is to be construed in the private sense. So it now becomes obvious that these two sentences are statements, respectively, of epistemological and analytical idealism. Considered as an account of the nature and limitations of science this is "a dominant epistemology that takes knowledge to be a construction placed directly on raw sense data by the mind" (Kuhn, p. 95).

It is, however, one of the most astonishing of all the many paradoxes of the history of ideas that such views should in our century be commonly proposed by those who cast themselves as hardline ideological commissars defending the pure doctrine of scientific enlightenment. For any idealism necessarily denies the very possibility of any knowledge of any independently existing objective reality; and such idealist misinterpretations were in fact originally developed and presented precisely in order to draw the teeth of science. This was why the Lutheran preacher Osiander supplied a neutralising Preface for the *De Revolutionibus* of Canon Copernicus. This was why Cardinal Bellarmino pressed a similar conception on Galileo. This was why the future Bishop Berkeley urged his own curiously modern philosophy of science upon contemporary Newtonian materialists (Popper: 2, pp. 97-119).

(b) The second remarkable merit is Lenin's insistence upon the solipsistic implications of idealism. Again eschewing any word-for-word repetition of Mach or Pearson, and of Lenin's comments thereon, consider once more those two sentences from the young Ayer. How on his own stated principles can he know that there is anybody else but Ayer? For people are a (very special) kind of physical object. If really all that Ayer can do is to predict the course of his own (private) sensory experience, and if this is really all that is involved in his belief in what he still perversely misdescribes as "the physical world", then he has no basis for any claim to know that there are any independently existing objects 'without the mind'. His proclaimed "belief in the reality of the physical world" is no more than a belief in the occurrence of his (private) sensory experience. Ayer writes always 'we' and 'our' when he cannot be entitled to write more than 'I' or 'my'. He has no business thus to help himself to the conclusions, which are in any case inconsistent with his wholesale general denials, that there are, and that he knows that there are, other people.

Someone may perhaps object, in the name of some Platonic-Cartesian view of the nature of man, that the real or essential person is incorporeal. Yet it will still have to be allowed that such creatures could know one another only through the media of their fleshly containers: "The human body is the best picture of the human soul" (Wittgenstein, p. 178: compare Flew: 6, Part 3).

Frankly solipsistic idealism is scarcely likely to have a wide appeal – least of all to social scientists or spokesmen for social science. We may recall Russell's story of his solipsist correspondent who wondered why so plausible a position had so few occupants! But it is just worth noticing that the most famous thesis of the later Wittgenstein – that, since language is essentially social, there could not be a logically private language – carries the implication that the solipsist could not intelligibly and consistently express his thesis even to himself (Wittgenstein, and compare Jones). Much more to the present point is to appreciate the insuperable obstacles to any would-be non-solipsistic idealism. To recognise another person either as a possible interlocutor or as a possible subject of discourse is, as I have just argued against Ayer, to identify an object 'without the mind'. And, furthermore, any conversation with such an object presupposes that we have a language in common. Yet we can have, and know that we have, a shared vocabulary only and precisely in so far as we are able to verify our mutual understandings by reference to public objects and public ongoings 'without the mind'. You and I can know that we mean the same by 'red', for instance, only in so far as at the end of the day we can both discern that we both accept the same specimens as standard (Flew: 1, II).

2. *Anthropology and Rationality*

Section 1 expounded Horton's distinction between two predicaments; and I challenged his assumption that, although we ought to have faith in the open and modern, it is impossible to refute the equally tenable closed and magical alternative. The emphasis there was on the nature of reality. I shall now examine a parallel thesis about rationality. It is put forward in two papers reprinted in a collection *Rationality*, edited by Bryan Wilson, in a series on 'Key Concepts in the Social Sciences'. These papers are by a Wittgensteinian philosopher, Peter Winch.

He begins by explaining why rationality is indeed a key concept in all the social sciences. The heart of the matter is that people, unlike anything else in the universe, may have and give reasons for what they do or abstain from doing; and to understand those reasons is the always necessary, but by no means always sufficient, condition of understanding the behaviour of people. (We noticed another aspect of this basic and distinguishing truth about the human sciences in Subsection 2(i) of Chapter 2.)

But then in his second paper, under the disquieting heading 'The Reality of Magic', Winch goes on to raise "certain difficulties about' Professor E. E. Evans-Pritchard's ... classic *Witchcraft, Oracles and Magic among the Azande*" (p. 78). These involve Winch faulting Evans-Pritchard for wanting to say "that the criteria applied in scientific experimentation constitute a true link between our ideas and an independent reality, whereas those characteristic of other systems of thought – in particular, magical methods of thought – do not" (pp. 82-3). Poor culture-bound Evans-Pritchard was, apparently, in error when he maintained that in their beliefs about witchcraft the Azande "attribute to phenomena supra-sensible qualities ... *which they do not possess*" (quoted p. 85; Winch's italics).

In a second part, on 'Our Standards and Theirs', Winch tries to justify this conclusion: "Something can appear rational to someone only in terms of *his* understanding of what is and is not rational. If *our* concept of rationality is a different one from his, then it makes no sense to say that anything either does or does not appear rational to *him* in *our* sense . . . MacIntyre seems to be saying that certain standards are taken as criteria of rationality because they *are* criteria of rationality. But whose?" (pp. 97-8; Winch's italics).

(i) About the first of the last two paragraphs I offer only two asides. First, this is by no means the only paper by a devout Wittgensteinian in which what would surely be better regarded as an attempted reduction to absurdity against some of the later ideas of the Master has instead been presented piously as an illuminating application. Compare, for instance, Norman Malcolm's now notorious attempt in the *Philosophical Review* for 1960 to create the Creator God of Abraham, Isaac and Israel out of the linguistic practices of believers: "This language game is played!" Second, it is, surely, too high a price for securing "the conception of God's reality" against any radical criticism from outside "the religious use of language" (p. 82), to make it impossible to deny the operation of witchcraft and the efficacy of magic? In the days of a more robust faith even the religious were happy to sing of how "the heathen in his blindness, bows down to wood and stone".

(a) About the second part of the exercise more has to be said. Winch's first claim here is true, because it is necessarily true. But in this correct interpretation it carries no disturbing implications. Certainly, and indeed necessarily, I can think only my own thoughts. But from this it does not follow, and it is in any case not true: either that I cannot share my thoughts with others; or that I cannot understand what other people are thinking, and sometimes know them to be in error. Whatever I (or you) think is necessarily my (or your) opinion. But it is as wrong as it is common to move, without further due reason given, from 'That is his opinion', to 'That is only his opinion'; where the second proposition is construed as denying that this opinion is known to be correct. (Compare Subsection 3(i) of Chapter 2.)

(b) Second, two people, or two cultures, can have two different concepts of this or that only in so far as there is considerable coincidence between one of these two concepts and the other. For the mere fact that the same vocable – 'rationality' say – is found to be used in two radically distinct ways indicates the subsistence, not of two concepts of rationality, but of two senses of the word 'rationality'. So, if there really are different concepts of rationality, then the differences between these cannot be either as total or as unbridgeable as Winch assumes.

(c) Third, Winch continues: "MacIntyre seems to be saying that certain standards are taken as criteria of rationality because they *are* criteria of rationality." Why, please, is this thought to be heinous? Suppose we discover that the Kachin word previously rendered as 'rationality' in fact refers to a wholly different concept, then this merely shows that we have been mistranslating. Suppose that the two terms are perfectly equivalent, then we have no alternatives to choose between. It is only if, though they are not perfectly equivalent, they do have a great deal in common that we are warranted to speak of two concepts of rationality. But to object now to the insistence that what they have in common – what makes them both concepts of rationality – is rationality is to align yourself with old Marshal Saxe. (It was he who, according to legend, wanted reassurance that the planet which we all call Uranus really is Uranus.)

(d) Fourth, we must be cautious about following Winch and others in accepting extensive and intractable disagreements as evidence that those who differ thus must have different concepts, and in particular different concepts of rationality. When, for instance, Soviet apologists insist that the 1968 reconquest of Czechoslovakia was not imperialism, it is tempting to suggest that they have a different concept of imperialism. Yet it is, of course, because we do mean the same things by the bad word 'imperialism' that they so bigotedly refuse to admit that the Great Russian Empire still exists – far more extensive now than ever under the old Tsars.

Nor must we overlook that people may be awkward or careless in their handling of a concept which they do in fact share with others more careful or more competent. The fact, for instance, that I get nearly all the logical exercises wrong is not good evidence that I am master of an alternative concept of deduction.

And, finally, even where there genuinely are conceptual cross-purposes we ought to be especially reluctant to trace these to widely different notions of rationality. Just because this notion is, or these notions are, central and fundamental to the human understanding of human beings, Winch-type theories constitute a threat to human solidarity. Groups with different concepts of rationality become to that extent non-communicating, mutually unintelligible sub-species. (Those who estimate the motives and intentions of our contemporary Radicals more highly than I, may be surprised to observe their inclination towards such truly divisive theories.)

(ii) Winch seems never to have asked himself how the first anthropologists in the field acquired their knowledge of the languages of their native informants. Yet the *English–Zande* or *English–Nuer Dictionary* did not descend from heaven, miraculously endowed with inexpugnable authority.

(a) This negative fact has vital implications, developed in two lucid and profound papers by Martin Hollis: "To understand native utterances the anthropologist must relate them to one another and to the world. To translate them into, let us say, English, he needs to relate some of them to the world, since, in relating an utterance to others he does not learn what it means, unless he already knows what the others mean" (p. 216). To acquire the bridgehead indispensable for further advance his "line of attack must be that a native sentence can be correctly translated by any English sentence which can be used in the same way in the same situations. ... Suppose he gets his bridgehead by pinning down the native counterparts of English sentences like 'Yes, this is a brown cow'. There are no native counterparts to pin down unless the natives perceive brown cows and assert that they do. For, since these are conditions for the English sentence meaning what it does, they are also conditions for any native sentence meaning the same. This is banal enough" (pp. 214-15).

Perhaps it is. Yet it is nevertheless sufficient to show that unless two cultures share at least some beliefs, and some ideas of truth and falsity and reality, there can be no communication between them. This would make them two distinct intellectual species, with no possibility of any anthropological understanding of either by the other. Both in fact and by definition the anthropologist is a human being studying others of his own kind. Only when he has achieved some measure of communication can he be ready to discern the most interesting of his problems. These arise exactly when and because his native informants have given him explanations of their conduct or of the working of their institutions which he finds unintelligible, or which – thanks perhaps to the fact that he comes from a culture which in at least this one respect must be superior – he knows to be false. In Chapter 2 I argued that the general idealism, and the particular denial of any knowable difference between reality and 'reality', which the sociologico-critics display as the prize of their sociological sophistication, are in fact incompatible with sociology in general, and with the sociology of knowledge in particular. Here now in Chapter 3 I am maintaining that the standardless relativism which Winch and others parade as the trophy of their unethnocentric anthropological enlightenment also leaves little or no room for the very studies upon which they think to found it.

Two or three examples will fix the cruces in mind. Take – with MacIntyre – tabu. This raises a problem for the anthropologist only because he cannot recognise tabu as an adequate reason for abstaining from anything. If he did he would, at least in this area, have abandoned his professional vocation and – as Wilson suggests, but is too fastidious to say in such crude words – gone native. Or consider totem. It is only in so far as we can recognise similarities between the general tribal usage of the word 'pontoxil', and the usage of our word 'porcupine', that we are perplexed when some of our tribe insist on saying that they just are pontoxil. Or again, consider – with Gellner – cases in which it is vital to the working of an institution that something or someone should be thought by the participants to possess some characteristic which it or he does not in fact possess. Thus it is part of the Berber concept of igurramen that these privileged yet functionally important persons are selected, and consequently endowed with most of their essential igurramen characteristics, by God. Yet it is because, and only because, the anthropologist appreciates that this belief is not true that he can and must raise the question how in actual fact they are selected. Gellner gives the answer: "What appears to be *vox Dei* is in reality *vox populi*" (p. 44). Winch's anthropologist, committed to the profoundly obscurantist doctrine that no one is ever objectively right or wrong about anything, could see no problems.

(b) In his second contribution Hollis continues: "The notions of truth and falsehood cannot be separated from the notion of logical reasoning. . . . An anthropologist does not know what he can say in the native language, unless he also knows what he cannot say. (That is why it is much easier to work with a native informant who can say 'No' to a question, than with a set of texts, which cannot.) . . . The anthropologist must find the word for 'No,' and to do so must assume that the natives share (at least partly) his concepts of identity, contradiction and inference" (p. 231). If there really are different concepts of rationality, then the common element which makes them all concepts of rationality must be or include whatever is essential for learning any language, and hence for determining what anyone is saying about anything. (Compare Subsection 3(iii) of Chapter 2.)

3.   *The Primacy of Untheoretical Discourse.*

Winch's standardless relativism refers in the first instance to the social sciences, and to anthropology in particular. *The Structure of Scientific Revolutions* presents similar doctrine in the context of the natural sciences. I shall not say much about Kuhn: partly just because he is primarily concerned with the natural rather than the social sciences; but mainly because he has recently been dealt with very faithfully by others. I am glad to recommend Roger Trigg's *Reason and Commitment* (pp. 99-118), Hugo Meynell's article, 'Science, the Truth and Thomas Kuhn' (*Mind*, vol. LXXXIV, no. 333, 1975), and John Watkins in Lakatos and Musgrave. It is, nevertheless, to the present point to remark that Kuhn himself as an historian of ideas – and thus as a kind of social scientist – cannot consistently maintain those characteristic notions which he believes that his studies justify.

(i) Giving his 'Reflections on my Critics' Kuhn writes: "Granting that neither theory of a historical pair is true, they nonetheless seek a sense in which the later is a better approximation to the truth. I believe that nothing of that sort can be found." Like our sociologico-critics he believes that it is (nearer to) the objective truth to deny that there is any such truth; and so, like them, he derides those who "wish . . . to compare theories as representations of nature, as statements about 'what is really out there' " (Lakatos and Musgrave, p. 265).

But, of course, while Kuhn is actually doing historical work he has to recognise that some scientists offer more or less good reasons for or against even what he calls paradigms, and that some paradigms are either more fruitful or themselves nearer the truth than others. Thus, in discussing paradigm changes –

shifts of allegiance, that is, from one to another of two supposedly incommensurable theoretical structures not suscept-ible of any independent critical appraisal – Kuhn tells us: "Because scientists are reasonable men, one or another argu-ment will ultimately persuade many of them. But there is no single argument that can or should persuade them all." The second of these two statements is, apparently, being mistaken to prove that really there is no room for reason. Again, in the same context, Kuhn says: "Something must make at least a few scientists feel that the new proposal is on the right track. . . ." (Kuhn, p. 157). How odd it is that he never asks himself: 'On the right track for where? What are the scientists trying to do?' Kuhn is here like those who tell us – oh so knowingly – that science is not concerned to discover truth, because scientists commend certain theories as fruitful rather than as true. Yet what is this good fruit if it is neither truth nor some better approximation to it?

(ii) Again in his 'Reflections' Kuhn writes: "The . . . compari-son of two successive theories demands a language into which at least the empirical consequences of both can be translated without loss or change . . . that theories can be compared by recourse to a basic vocabulary consisting entirely of words which are attached to nature in ways that are unproblematic and, to the extent necessary, independent of theory." Kuhn denies that any "such vocabulary is available. . . . Successive theories are thus . . . incommensurable" (Lakatos and Musgrave, pp. 266-7).

But now, in what vocabulary does Kuhn or any other historian of science begin to describe one of these paradigm changes? Obviously he begins by employing only the ordinary untechnical and untheoretical vocabulary of whatever language he himself is working in. Nor does he find it impossibly difficult to describe the crucial observations and experiments in neutral terms, even though the protagonists perhaps relied on their own loaded technicalities. When he wants to introduce any of the theoretical notions of either of the rival paradigms he will do this, as the original sponsors of these paradigms must at some stage themselves have done, by explaining these novelties in the untheoretical and untechnical terms of the ordinary vocabulary – supplementing his explanations in words with various sorts of showing as and when necessary.

Suppose someone now suggests that even an ordinary

untechnical vocabulary must be itself theoretically loaded, then our reply must be that it can be, and is, "to the extent necessary, independent of theory".[9] Certainly an everyday descriptive term, 'sunrise' for instance, may be said to bear hidden theoretical overtones. Yet if it is construed, as it usually is, as ostensively definable, then these normally unnoticed associations cannot be rated as part of the meaning of the word. For nothing, surely, which is ostensively definable can be in any relevant way theoretically loaded?

The anthropologist, as we have seen, has to start by establishing some vocabulary shared with his tribe. It is only upon this basis that he can begin to ask his distinctively anthropological questions. In the same way the historian of science investigating paradigm changes has to have some vocabulary shared with both his tribes if he is to begin to understand what the conflict was about, and perhaps to hope to appreciate its development better than its participants did. If the rival systems really were irredeemably opaque to one another they would both, presumably, be equally or more opaque to the latter-day historian: "We are suitors for agreement from everyone else, because we are fortified with a ground common to all" (Kant: 2, I(i) 19).

4   Sociology and Equality

"Social inequality has always been one of the major preoccupations of sociology – largely, perhaps, because of the strong moral commitment which many sociologists bring to their work." So say Penguin Education, in heavy type, in introducing a collection of readings on *Social Inequality*, edited by André Béteille. No doubt there is something in their suggested explanation. But I shall show in the present chapter that there are also strong occupational temptations to seduce sociologists into believing both that people naturally are, and that ideally they ought to be, more equal than – for better or for worse – actually is the case.

1.   *Two Senses of 'a Social Problem'*

The Editor, who is a Jawaharlal Nehru Fellow and Reader in Sociology at the University of Delhi, opens his Introduction with the statement:

> Social inequality is a broad and general problem, one which is present in all contemporary societies. In the past, societies have differed greatly in their attitudes to inequality, but in the modern world it would be hard indeed to find any society whose members are indifferent to the problem. The industrial societies of the USA and the USSR alike justify their respective systems by the argument that they provide the best opportunities for real social equality. For the more 'backward' societies, the chief appeal of industrialization is the promise it holds of bringing inequality under control. (p. 9)

The Editor continues: "The contributions selected here deal, on the whole, with sociologically significant problems which are (or can be) discussed in terms of empirically testable propositions" (p. 10).

The first distinction which we need to make is between two fundamentally different interpretations of such expressions as 'the problem of social inequality'. In the one the questions are scientific: we want to know why various sorts of social inequality, or whatever else, have in fact arisen and do in fact continue. There is no necessary implication that all or even any of these differences are bad. But in the other interpretation the point of calling something a social problem is just to express the belief that the world would be a better place without it. There may be no suggestion of any relevant insufficiency of knowledge or understanding.

It may be both deplorable and perhaps unusual, but it is neither inconsistent nor sociologically unprofessional, for someone to be concerned with the problems (in the scientific sense) of social inequality, without believing that all social inequality is wrong. This seems in fact to be the position of the first contributor, Ralf Dahrendorf. For he quotes with approval some words of Immanuel Kant, who rated "inequality among men" a "rich source of much that is evil, but also of everything that is good" (p. 16). Again, albeit conversely, it is not inconsistent, although it might be thought on some other ground outrageous, to list in your miscellany of contemporary social problems both oldtime unpolitical stealing and the new look, politicised, student hooliganism; while nevertheless insisting that neither of these particular two provides scope for useful and novel sociological inquiry.[10] It is, surely, in the second and normative sense that another contributor to the present volume – himself presumably an Afrikaner in exile – speaks of "The 'white problem' in South Africa" (p. 319).

Equipped with this distinction between two senses of the expression 'the problem of social inequality' we can see that the second of the two passages quoted from the Editor refers to questions of the first, the scientific sort: "sociologically significant problems . . . discussed in terms of empirically testable propositions". The first passage has, on the other hand, to be construed in the second way. Yet, once the ambiguity has been identified and explicated, we shall want to query the two suggestions: that all men now see social inequality as a great evil, if not as the greatest of evils; and that it is in the service of this supposed new universal ideal, rather than in rising expectations of escaping from poverty, that the peoples of the backward countries demand industrialisation.

It is here significant, for instance, that in his widely acclaimed treatise on *Inequality* the Harvard sociologist Christopher Jencks frequently laments that his compatriots do not share his own passion for every form of equality: "Unfortunately. . . . Income inequality is not yet perceived as a major social problem, much less as a cause of other social ills" (Jencks, p. 232: compare Nisbet, 'The Pursuit of Equality', *The Public Interest*, Spring 1974).

2. *Aristotelian Versus Enlightenment Norms*

(i) In the article mentioned Dahrendorf proceeds to quote Aristotle's *Politics*: "It is thus clear that there are by nature free men and slaves, and that servitude is agreeable and just for the latter. . . . Equally, the relation of the male to the female is by nature such that one is superior and the other inferior, one dominates and the other is dominated"; and, furthermore, as "the poets say, 'It is just that Greeks rule over Barbarians', because the Barbarian and the slave are by nature the same". Dahrendorf comments: "Now this is just the attitude that makes impossible a sociological treatment of the problem, that is, an explanation of inequality in terms of specifically social factors expressed in propositions capable of being empirically tested" (p. 18).

We have to appreciate both why and how far this comment is right. The correct point is that, if something really is a matter of either natural necessity or natural impossibility, then there is no room for an extra and sociological explanation. This remains true notwithstanding that it is false to say that any of the three cases cited by Aristotle are of this kind. That they are not is best shown by the very fact that Aristotle is in this way appealing to the supposed dictates of nature. For he does this precisely and only in order as best he may to enforce those particular hierarchical social relationships which always are, in his view, proper – despite the too-familiar facts, which he himself is among the first to recognise and to bewail, that they are not always observed. If these approved superiorities and approved subordinations really were matters of natural necessity and of natural impossibility; then exhortations, or reproaches, or appeals to what is alleged to constitute natural justice, would be all equally otiose and inept (Flew: 4, pp. 94-108).

Once we are seized of this it is also clear that Aristotle will have to be taken as appealing: not to some putative natural necessity making it sheerly impossible for Greeks to be ruled by Barbarians, or for women to give orders to men, or for some people to be anything but slaves; but to the alleged fact that the natural capacities and incapacities, the natural inclinations and disinclinations, of women, or Barbarians, or whatever, are such that it must be wrong for them to occupy positions other than those to which Aristotle proposes that they ought to be allocated. But now, in so far as this is what he was saying, he was not, as Dahrendorf maintained, closing the door on sociological inquiry. Given that the natural facts are what Aristotle holds them to be, and supposing that we also accept his normative commitments, then the questions which arise will be questions of how and how far people contrive or fail to achieve or to maintain their supposedly proper positions.

(ii) Having thus, I suggest, misread the implications of Aristotle's position, Dahrendorf proceeds to contrast it with another. This derives from Rousseau's famous essay of 1754 on *The Origin of Inequality among Men and Whether It is Legitimated by Natural Laws.* Dahrendorf comments: "A straight road leads from such reflections to the Declaration of the Rights of Man and the Citizen of 1789: 'Men are born and remain free and equal in rights. Social differences, therefore, can only be based on general utility' " (p. 21).[11] (No doubt the development was continuous. Yet it is scarcely a straight route which proceeds from Dijon to Paris by way of Philadelphia: "We hold these truths to be self-evident, that all men are created equal, that they are endowed by their Creator with certain unalienable rights, and that among these are life, liberty, and the pursuit of happiness.")

The moral drawn by Dahrendorf from the French Declaration is: "that the question of the origin of inequality was now phrased in a new . . . manner. If men are by nature equal in rank, where do social inequalities come from? If all men are born free and equal in rights, how can we explain that some are rich and others poor, some respected and others ignored, some powerful and others in servitude? Once the question was posed in these terms, only a sociological answer was possible" (p. 21).

Now, certainly, once it is appreciated that there is any gap between whatever social positions people do actually occupy and the positions which they might have occupied, then questions do arise which demand sociological answers. How, that is, does it come about that people occupy the positions which they do in fact occupy; and not others? Yet this, as we have already seen, applies equally to the quoted statements of Aristotle, once these are correctly understood. In a note to the present passage Dahrendorf himself hints that the distinctive positive affirmations of the eighteenth century were not really essential to the argument: "here, as so often, what was historically necessary is logically superfluous" (pp. 21-2n.).

What Dahrendorf altogether fails to bring out is the crucial and fundamental difference between claims about an equality of rights and claims about an equality of talents or of inclinations. To assert the former is not the same as, nor does it logically presuppose, an assertion of the latter; or the other way about. Those who drafted the two great Declarations were concerned to affirm equalities only of rights. They were not so foolish as to believe, nor to require others to believe: either that at birth we all are in fact equal in our potentialities; or that this false contention is the essential logical basis for any affirmation of equal rights. (Compare Sjöstrand.) So Stalin was simply missing the point of the American dream when he protested to a visiting American Senator: "You believe that men are equal. I know that they are not."

That the French Declaration was concerned with an equality of rights is obvious. Precisely that is what the first of the two sentences quoted by Dahrendorf says. The second too is concerned only with what ideally ought to be the case, not with what actually is so. The point is, not that social differences always in fact are, but that they always ought to be, based on (justifiable, that is to say, by reference to) general utility. And those who propounded and prospered under the slogan 'La carrière ouverte aux talents' certainly had no inclination to believe that nature had in fact distributed equal shares of talent to all. The meaning of the passage quoted from the American Declaration is perhaps a shade less manifest and unequivocal. But if we read the whole sentence, and not the first two clauses alone, it surely becomes clear that the final claims about unalienable rights are intended to explicate the phrase which is too often torn out of context: "that all men are created equal".

3. *Limits of Sociological Explanation*

The note mentioned already in Subsection 2(ii) continues: "once the question of the origin of inequality is posed in a sociological way (i.e. without recourse to natural inequalities), its answer has nothing to do with whether or not men are by nature equal or unequal" (p. 22n.). This is an obscure and confused statement. The obscurity and the confusion derive, I think, from Dahrendorf's failure to seize either of the main points made in the previous two sections.

Certainly the strictly sociological questions about social inequality have no necessary connections with the normative stances either of Aristotle, or of the Enlightenment, or of such contemporary egalitarian ultras as Christopher Jencks. We can – and good sociologists such as Jencks do – raise and press questions about the actual origin and persistence of social rankings without thereby either presupposing or implying that any such rankings either are, or are not, right and proper.

But it is wrong to suggest that the possibilities of sociological explanation cannot be circumscribed by the subsistence of natural, as opposed to social, inequalities between different people and groups of people. For in so far as "something really is a matter of either natural necessity or natural impossibility", then truly, as I argued in Section 2, "there is no room for an extra and sociological explanation".

Exactly this last was what Dahrendorf himself accepted and assumed when he urged that Aristotle shuts the door in the face of sociology by his insistence that the relative rankings of men or women, masters or slaves, Greeks or Barbarians, are all determined by nature. Our disagreement was: that Dahrendorf apparently mistook Aristotle to be saying that the natural, as opposed to social, determination here is such as to make it impossible for anyone to fulfil any but their actual role; whereas I construe Aristotle as holding that, while non-social nature determines our several initial capacities and inclinations, these in their turn determine, not what our several social roles in fact are, but what they ought to be. In neither case could it be right either to seek or to propound a sociological explanation for whatever in actual fact happens to be the outcome of purely non-social causes.

It is overtime to descend from the abstract and the theoretical nearer to the concrete and practical. Yet, just because we are moving towards some very topical and much controverted issues, some precautionary preliminaries are needed. First, my own contention, against Aristotle, is: that he was right on the point of fact, that individuals, and even some classes of individuals – though not all the three particular classes which he specified! – do vary considerably in their initial capacities and inclinations; but that he was wrong on the point of philosophical logic, since conclusions of right – conclusions, that is, about what ought or ought not to be done – cannot validly be deduced from propositions stating only what is in fact the case. If the former were thus validly deducible from the latter then it would, by the definition of 'valid deductive argument', be self-contradictory to deny the one while asserting the other. It never is. For instance: it is not contradictory – although it may well be on other grounds obnoxious – to allow that someone is blind, or congenitally stupid, or a man, or a woman; and then to take this fact either as a qualification or as a disqualification for the award of some privilege.

The second thing to notice is that claims about the capacities and inclinations of classes of people are most likely – unless these classes themselves are deliberately specified in terms of the possession of the particular characteristics under discussion – to be claims about averages and ranges. But, as Plato saw when he wrote his classic attack on sexism,[12] we cannot validly infer any categorical conclusion about a particular member of a class from a general statement about the average characteristics of that class. You may live in a place where the average height is five foot ten, but this tells me nothing about your height. If any strictly logical fallacies deserve to be called the fallacies of racism, then it is this move, and the Naturalistic Fallacy described in the previous paragraph, which merit that description. For racism surely consists in holding it either for or against an individual that he happens to be a member of some particular well-favoured or ill-favoured racial category. And it is only by committing these two fallacies that we can pass in argument: from statements about what the average capacities and inclinations of particular racial categories are; to conclusions about how individual members of those categories ought to be treated.

4.   *Assumptions and Presumptions in Sociology*

(i) It is, I think, mainly because they have not grasped that these two forms of argument are unsound that so many people nowadays want to stifle investigation of possible differences in innate capacities and inclinations as between different racial groups. For if you reject the immoral moral doctrine that a person may properly be advantaged or disadvantaged on the ground of belonging to some particular racial group, and if you also believe that these fallacious forms of argument are valid, then you may very intelligibly reach the false conclusion that your moral stand against racism logically presupposes that there are no such average differences in innate capacities and inclinations. This leaves you ready to join the obscurantist chorus of protest and denunciation against anyone who dares to say that the evidence so far available appears to indicate that in fact there are. (But see Chapter 5 below.)

Sometimes well-intentioned, but always muddle-headed anxieties of this sort are in some measure responsible for the fact that so many sociologists assume that there is no call to consider any such unfashionable possibilities. Analogous anxieties also in part account for the similar but weaker reluctance to recognise such average differences as between non-racial social classes. But these muddles and inhibitions are intrusions into the domain of science. Our concern at present is with the support which such assumptions may receive, or may seem to receive, from the commitments proper to sociology itself.

(a) David Lane is a Lecturer in Sociology at the University of Essex. In his *The End of Inequality? Stratification under State Socialism* we read: "A characteristic of a democratic occupational structure is that leading and intellectual occupations are both desired and actually open to all children independently of their social background. One might expect, other things being equal, that the distribution of children in professional occupations would *not* vary with the occupation of their fathers" (p. 107: italics original).[13]

On the contrary: we may *not* expect this – except in so far as we can assume that there are not, even on average, any relevant natural (as opposed to socially determined) differences between the offspring of the various occupational groups considered in this comparison. If, for instance, there are genetically determined differences such that the offspring of those in "leading and intellectual occupations" have more of whatever may be the relevant innate abilities and inclinations than the offspring of those in trailing and unintellectual occupations; then the former will – all other things being equal – be disproportionately represented among the new generation in the "leading and intellectual occupations".

Now why should a sociologist be tempted, and tempted precisely as a sociologist, to overlook the possibility, indeed the actuality, of such innate differences? Obviously one most professional temptation lies in the fact that innate, as opposed to socially determined, differences cannot of their very nature be explained sociologically. (See Section 2, above.) Nor should this sophisticated temptation to occupational aggrandisement be too hastily dismissed as merely the analogue, at a rather more pretentious social level, of something obtrusively familiar among strongly unionised manual workers. For while it surely is this, there may also be more to it.

Allow that we do not always and everywhere know where to draw the line between nature and nurture; which in fact we do not. Then where we do not know, and until we do, it may be good heuristic policy for both the geneticists and the sociologists to investigate: for certainly neither will find whatever is the true explanation without looking for it. Whichever eventually succeeds becomes thereby entitled to annex that particular bit of intellectual real estate to the territories of their own science. But when and where they are playing it that way, it is important that everyone should realise exactly what the position is. In such cases, and until the game is up, the sociologists are at best entitled to presume, but not to assume, that the future belongs to them.

The nerve of this distinction is best displayed by reference to the presumption of innocence in the English Common Law. This is not the lunatic assumption that every accused is in fact innocent. It is the insistence that the onus of proof of guilt rests upon the prosecution. It is, therefore, not hypocritical for counsel to affirm belief in the presumption of innocence while privately believing, perhaps with decisive good reason, that the accused is in fact guilty. So to presume that people or groups are in fact naturally equal, is to insist that it is up to the geneticists and to the psychologists to prove that they are not; if they can.

The methodological presumption is certainly not the same as the corresponding assumption; since it is entirely possible, while still maintaining the former, to conclude that the latter is now known to be partially or wholly false (see Flew: 6, 1).

The reasons which Lane might offer for adopting such a presumption cannot, therefore, justify his unstated and perhaps even unnoticed assumption that there are no relevant natural differences. One sufficient objection is that it is known that there in fact are substantial and relevant natural differences, although their full extent and basis remain subject to legitimate dispute. That it is indeed known can for present purposes be sufficiently substantiated by quoting Jencks, who is in his objectives about as extreme an egalitarian as we could find: "The evidence . . . underlines the limited value of equalizing 'opportunity' without equalizing anything else. Students are not all equally talented, equally ambitious, or equally hard working. A system which provides everyone with equal opportunity will ensure that the more talented, ambitious, and diligent succeed, while others fail. . . . The fact that this happens does not prove that the students' educational opportunities were unequal; it proves that equal opportunity is not enough to ensure equal results" (p. 37).

(b) Lane's failure to take account of any natural as opposed to socially determined human differences is not unusual, but typical. An even more striking example is provided by Raymond Boudon, author of *The Logic of Sociological Explanation.* (That was, perhaps surprisingly, yet another exercise in Penguin Education.) Boudon's *Education, Opportunity, and Social Inequality* is introduced by Seymour Martin Lipset as the work of "France's leading sociological theorist and methodologist"; who, fittingly, "holds the chair at Paris once occupied by Durkheim" (pp. vi and vii).

On the first page of his Preface Boudon defines 'inequality of educational opportunity (IEO)' as "differences in level of educational attainment according to social background". He draws the consequence that "a society is characterized by a certain amount of IEO if, for instance, the probability of going to college is smaller for a worker's son than for a lawyer's son". 'Inequality of social opportunity (ISO)' is defined similarly. The parallel consequence is that "a society is characterized by a certain amount of ISO if the probability of reaching a high social status is smaller for the former child than for the latter" (p. xi). Having thus defined his terms Boudon states: "My primary objective is to attempt to explain why the tremendous educational development that occurred in all Western societies following World War II had so little impact on equality; that is, why IEO has decreased so little and why ISO, in spite of this development, does not appear to have decreased at all" (p. xv).

He would be rash indeed who suggested that the whole of the answer to Boudon's problem is to be found in the field of genetics, rather than of social science. Yet this rash claim, which no one has made, is far, far less reckless and less blinkered than the contrary assumption built into Boudon's fundamental definitions. Without apparently noticing what he has done, and certainly without ever offering so much as a sentence in attempted justification, Boudon takes it as absolutely for granted from the beginning that there are no significant, hereditarily determined differences in either talent, temperament or inclination. If there are any differences in educational attainment between the child of a lawyer, or a group of lawyers' children, and the child of a teamster, or a group of teamsters' children; then for Boudon this is by definition a sufficient reason to raise the cry: 'Its unfair. It's all due to unequal educational opportunity.'

It is again symptomatic of the total and uncritical environmentalism so widespread at this time among sociologists that, in the main review of the week in *New Society* (23 May 1974), Alan Little quoted both of Boudon's basic definitions without noticing – much less either questioning or trying to vindicate – the grossly counterfactual assumption contained therein. It was still no sociologist, but the psychologist H. J. Eysenck, who, two weeks later in a letter, pointed out that "Boudon constructs a whole model of educational and social opportunity . . . very much as if every child . . . were an identical twin to every other child" (6 June 1974). By contrast the sociologist reviewer had ended almost on his knees before such "originality in approach, a mixture of creative imagination and intellectual rigour, a continual juxtaposition of logic and fact, statistical sophistication, theoretical acumen and wide reading".

Rousseau has been picked out as the first father of the sociological study of inequality. It is therefore apt to emphasise, as Dahrendorf does, that Rousseau himself insisted on the reality of both natural and socially determined differences. "There are", he underlined, "two kinds of inequality . . . one, which I call natural or physical . . . consists in a difference of age, health, bodily strength, and the qualities of the mind or of the soul; and another, which may be called moral or political inequality, because it depends on a kind of convention, and is established, or at least authorized, by the consent of men" (p. 160).

(ii) Because it is, apparently, so easy to confound contentions about what supposedly is the case with claims about what ought to be, all assertions or assumptions or presumptions about factual equality are apt to be misconstrued as either being or supporting the corresponding egalitarian norms. But the most seductive form which this temptation here takes refers to a fundamental of sociological inquiry. For it quite certainly is the business of sociology as a science to explain how and why the second of Rousseau's two kinds of inequality arises, and persists.

Social equality of this kind thus serves as an ideal standard, all departures from which require explanation. To serve legitimately in this role such social equality must not, of course, be so defined as to preclude the subsistence of important natural inequalities. (This negative requirement really is, pace Boudon, part of the logic of sociological explanation!) Social equality as a theoretical (as opposed to normative) ideal standard thus fulfils a function parallel to that of the first law of motion in physics. That law does not pretend to describe what physicists have observed to happen; much less prescribe what somebody thinks ought to happen. But where and in so far as we do observe bodies not to be behaving in the way in which they would behave if they were subject to that law *and to that law only* – and that is as near as makes no matter always – there we are as physicists committed to accounting for these deviations actually observed in terms of other "impressed forces". So it is with equality in societies. It is not that we always, or even ever, observe the ideal limiting case of total and universal social (as opposed to natural) equality. It is that we are always as sociologists committed to explaining all those defections from it which we do observe.

Sociologists, therefore, are by profession required to be sharply sensitive to the existence of social (as opposed to natural) inequalities. They may well be tempted to misinterpret the ideal limiting case of total and universal social (as opposed to natural) equality. This does indeed have a fundamental place in the framework of sociological thought. The temptation is to misconstrue it in that place as if it were a normative ideal sufficiently vindicated by that way of thinking. Yet to do this would be about as sensible as for a physicist to assume that all bodies ideally ought to be either at rest or in uniform motion in a right line.

5   The Jensen Uproar

1.   *The Proposition and the Opposition*

In the winter of 1969 the *Harvard Educational Review* published a long article by Professor Arthur Jensen of the University of California at Berkeley. In this article Jensen reviewed the psychological evidence bearing upon the question 'How Much Can We Boost IQ and Scholastic Achievement?' The original publication occasioned an enormous coast-to-coast brouhaha. From the monstrously misnamed Students for a Democratic Society (S.D.S.) there came a wave of tyre-slashing, slogan-painting, telephoned or shouted abuse and threats, and strident demands to "Fire" or even to "Kill Jensen". The campaign went on to embrace two further favourite enemies: the Harvard psychologist Richard Herrnstein, author of *IQ in the Meritocracy*; and, a little out of place, the Nobel Prize-winning physicist, William Shockley. The spillover in Britain included: a happily not very severe physical assault on the psychologist H. J. Eysenck at the London School of Economics, executed by a group said to consist of Maoist student toughs from Birmingham; the gazumping by the University of Leeds on its offer of an honorary degree to Shockley; and the decision by the National Union of Students (N.U.S.) by all available means to prevent any meeting in any British institution of tertiary education to be addressed by a speaker deemed by the local N.U.S. branch to be "racist or fascist".

Jensen has since republished the offending article, along with several shorter contributions in the same area, as a book on *Genetics and Education*. The sixty-seven-page Preface giving the author's own soberly factual account of the whole deplorable affair shows, among other things, how many of those who used to say that they approved the ends but abhorred the means of Senator Joe McCarthy were speaking the exact opposite of the truth (p. 19). The psychological conclusion which has given so much offence was incongruously, though no doubt with good reason, cautious: "So all we are left with are various lines of evidence, no one of which is definitive alone, but which, taken all together, make it a not unreasonable hypothesis that genetic factors are strongly implicated in the average Negro–white intelligence difference" (p. 163).

The word 'intelligence' is here given a technical definition in terms of I.Q. tests; and so those differences, which are of course only and precisely differences on average, just are the differences which are in fact found in actual achievement on these present tests. For the geneticist, Jensen maintains, the right form of question is: "How much of the variation (i.e. individual differences) in a particular trait or characteristic that we observe or measure (i.e. the phenotype) in a given population can we account for in terms of variation in the genetic factors (i.e. the genotype) affecting the development of the characteristic?" (p. 85). The fact that hereditary and environmental factors interact makes it difficult, but certainly not impossible, to answer questions of this form. Nor is it the point in the present context to complain that I.Q. tests are culturally skewed: "To the extent that a test is not 'culture free' or 'culture fair', it will result in a lower heritability measurement. It makes no more sense to say that intelligence tests do not really measure intelligence but only *developed* intelligence than to say that scales do not really measure a person's weight but only the weight he has acquired by eating. An 'environment free' test of intelligence makes as much sense as a 'nutrition free' scale for weight" (pp. 117-18: italics original).

Whether there are in fact average phenotypical or genotypical differences between different races or racial groups, either in intelligence as thus technically defined, or in intelligence in the ordinary sense, or in any other kind of inclination or capacity, are all scientific questions. I am not qualified, and I shall not try, to do more about these than indicate some reasons why it is most unlikely that the true answer is 'No'. But the Jensen controversy raises other issues, some of which are on any reckoning philosophical. Also, all good citizens of the republic of letters must be concerned about any threat to free inquiry; as well as about defections from proper academic standards, and the courteous decencies of civilised discussion.

2. *An Essay in Penguin Education*

Such more general issues are what we might hope to find treated in a work whose Editors assert: "In planning this book we have attempted to step back from the debate itself and look at the concepts which underlie it. This involves a close examination of the key ideas – intelligence, race, heredity, and environment – as well as following some of the implications of the evidence for our complex, heterogeneous society." Unfortunately this promise is not kept in Penguin Education's *Race, Culture and Intelligence*, edited by K. Richardson and D. Spears. These Editors, both of the Open University, have instead orchestrated a collective onslaught upon what their Open University colleague Donald Swift calls "the blinkered scientism of the Jensenist heresy" (p. 156).

One essential conspicuously not even attempted is "a close examination of the key ideas" of race and racism. No contributor, for instance, tries to explicate the distinction between race and nationality, as any precursors in a Penguin Special in the thirties certainly would have done. So nothing is said which would bring out the absurdity of a recent reference to the Race Relations Board by Robyn Lewis of Pwllheli, a Vice-President of Plaid Cymru: he complained that Reg Prentice's charge that trades unions were welshing on their solemn and binding social contract was "blatantly racialist and abusive" (*Daily Telegraph*, 22 March 1975). Nor will the reader find any light on the perhaps more difficult question whether Israel's Law of Return is correctly characterised as racialist: on the one hand people of almost all physical types qualify for the dangerous privilege of Israeli citizenship; on the other hand this qualification does descend by right of birth from the mother, and irrespective of either her nationality or that of her spouse.

(i) (a) The Editors set the tone in their Foreword, where in their second sentence they snarl at the position of Arthur Jensen and H. J. Eysenck, "ostensibly vindicated by dispassionate appeal to scientific evidence" (p. 9). They keep it up later with talk of the "academic posturings" with which the hated heretics present "rationalizations for views already latent in society" (p. 146). One characteristic move is to offer a speculation in the functionalist sociology of knowledge as if that speculation, were it well founded, would be by itself sufficient to discredit whatever is in question. Thus John Daniels and Vincent Houghton, of – respectively – Nottingham University and Huddersfield Polytechnic, assert that in the Second World War: "Psychometry was built into the war-machine with an important psychological role to play – to keep the conscripted soldiers thinking that in the 'democratic army' everyone had a 'fair' deal" (pp. 68–9; and compare p. 18).

Maybe this employment of psychometry was nothing but a front and a fraud; or maybe not. My complaint is that these authors neither parade, nor refer to, any evidence which might justify their insertion of the sneer quotes. Nor, of course, do they, or any other contributors, ever blackleg by being so scientifically curious, or so self-critical, or simply so un-self-righteous, as to think up some equally unflattering ætiological or functional suggestions to account for, and by the same bogus token to discredit, the enterprise in which they are themselves engaged. A speculative counter-offensive could be salutary. What offers?

(b) It is, again, altogether typical that no contributor, from the beginning of the book to the end, provides us with any evidence of their ever having addressed themselves directly to Jensen's own work. Although the Index – which is, incidentally, incomplete here – registers nineteen references to Jensen and Jensenism, only W. K. Bodmer, Professor of Genetics at Oxford, manages to repeat words written by the condemned heresiarch. Even then, corrupted perhaps by the company he has chosen to keep, he cites these as "Eysenck quotes", giving no page reference, title, or publisher for either author (pp. 109, 111-12, and 113). It is, therefore, though ill done, fitting that when finally the Editors do disclose the title and place of publication of the article which touched off the whole affair it is in a list of possible Further Reading, at the end of their statement of Conclusions (p. 195). Typical too, is the shoddiness which allows contributors to omit all identifying particulars of research papers to which they appeal for support (for example, pp. 26, 103, 107, 108 and 137). Others even get away with a reference to (unnamed) "geneticists in a recent article in the *Scientific American* (p. 76). It is ominous when such work is published by university teachers, and by teachers of teachers.

(c) Similarly revealing, and similarly portentous, is the abysmal quality of so much of the argument. Thus Daniels and Houghton say, of a "system of graded meritocratic assessment of social roles", that, "It is hard to see how the grading system can be retained when a guarantee of job opportunity can no longer be given" (p. 78). But no, it is easy to see. What is a bit embarrassing is then to have to point out that no one is going to choose an unqualified person as their own doctor, or as the captain of their own ship, for no better reason than that there happen to be more people around with medical degrees, or with Master's Certificates, than there are jobs for them. The same two proudly present, as knock-down decisive proof of the unimportance of heredity, this: "if 80 per cent of adult performance is directly dependent on genetic inheritance, how have the styles of our lives and the patterns of our thinking changed to the extent that they have? . . . there is no answer to this question" (p. 74). Yes, there is. But to appreciate that answer you need to be master, as this precious pair manifestly are not, of the elementary distinction between necessary and sufficient conditions.

(d) A final sign of shabby times is provided by John Rex, Professor of Sociology in the University of Warwick. He writes: "One significant phenomenon . . . is the body of ideas associated with the words ecology, conservation, pollution, etc. In this latter case human political judgement is no longer considered, even as an intervening variable. The ills of the world are simply explained as being due to inexorable scientific laws" (p. 176).

You will surely have to read that one again before you can believe your eyes. For, of course, what all the fuss about ecology, conservation and pollution is actually about, precisely is what generally is not, but could be, and should be, done. I suggest that Rex is victim here of motivated psychic blindness. What is so awkward for Rex the Radical about the evils which concern conservationists is that these are evils which with all the ill will in the world he can scarcely attribute exclusively to capitalism, or propose to cure by the total nationalisation of everything. In fact, for instance, the arch-socialists of the Russian Empire unite with the arch-capitalists of Japan to destroy the remaining species of whales.

Be that, however, as it may. For anyone concerned for education, and for educational standards, the significant thing is that a leading sociologist is here without a qualm presenting as a significant phenomenon something which a moment's thought would tell him, or anyone else, is false. What kind of students can be being selected for, or produced in, the Department of Sociology at Warwick if such flagrant falsehoods are there, apparently, allowed to pass unchallenged?

In an article referring directly only to the North American side of the present affair Michael Scriven, a philosopher in the University of California at Berkeley, develops a thesis which, it is now clear, applies to Britain too. This article was first solicited by the *Harvard Educational Review,* refused as insufficiently hostile to Jensen, but eventually published in the *Review of Educational Research* for 1970. The thesis is that the whole uproar reveals appalling educational neglect and failure.

(ii) Suppose that at last we really do "step back from the debate itself and look at the concepts which underlie it". Then the first and most fundamental question arising is: 'If so, so what? Why is it thought to matter so much whether the conclusion tentatively stated by Jensen is true or not?'

The contributor who comes nearest to bringing this out as a question, and to offering some answer, is, perhaps surprisingly, Rex. This nearest is not very near. What Rex says is, first, that what the scientist "does when he rates individuals or groups of individuals on a scale of measured intelligence is to say and to predict that one group of individuals rather than another should have privileges. . . . Scientific observations have political implications and the scientist should beware that that which he reveals may contribute to, or ease, human suffering." A little later Rex continues, second: "UNESCO and a distinguished line of social scientists who have worked to expose fallacies of racism, have always recognized that there is ground for supposing that there is a genetic component in measured intelligence. . . . What they have disputed is that these differences are so great that manipulation of the environment is not capable of fundamental-ly altering them" (p. 169).

(a) What Rex actually says in the first of the two passages quoted is that to rate some people higher than others "on a scale of measured intelligence is to say . . . that one group of individuals rather than another should have privileges". This is false. It is not to *say* anything of the sort. It would be perfectly consistent, although it might well be thought to be silly or in some other way misguided, to say that Ying has a far higher I.Q. than Yang, while simultaneously insisting, either that both should be treated in exactly the same way, or that Yang ought to have privileges not vouchsafed to Ying. Think for instance of Shockley's notorious but surely consistent proposal that people with an I.Q. of less than 100 should be paid, at the rate of a thousand dollars for every point below, to get sterilised.[14] Or think of the alternative society described in the eleventh century of our era by the Chinese poet Su Tung-p'o:

> Families, when a child is born
> Want it to be intelligent.
> I, through intelligence,
> Having wrecked my whole life,
> Only hope the baby will prove
> Ignorant and stupid.
> Then he will crown a tranquil life
> By becoming a Cabinet Minister (Waley, p. 98).

The distinction between *ought* and *is* is fundamental here. This Jensen, unlike most of his critics, fully appreciates: "realization of the moral ideal of equality proclaimed by the Declaration of Independence, of course, does not depend upon either phenotypic or genotypic equality of individuals' psychological characteristics" (p. 57, and compare p. 329. See also Eysenck, pp. 9-12). Contrast with this clear statement the long executive resolution, apparently adopted with virtually no dissent by the New Orleans conference in 1970, in which it is said: "The American Anthropological Association repudiates statements now appearing in the United States that Negroes are biologically and in innate mental ability inferior to whites, and reaffirms the fact that there is no scientifically established evidence to justify the exclusion of any race from the rights guaranteed by the Constitution of the United States" (quoted Jensen, p. 38; and compare, again, Chapter II of Sjöstrand). The crux is that the Signers were making claims about certain rights which all men *ought* to have, which claims neither entail nor presuppose that it *is* the case that all men are hereditarily equal in their talents or inclinations.

It has been suggested, by among others Michael Schleifer in *Philosophy* for October 1973 ('The Flew–Jensen Uproar', vol. 48, no. 186), that the position of the previous two paragraphs is "much too dogmatic". Certainly, as I have myself every reason to know, there has been philosophical debate about this

Humean antithesis. See, for instance, Hudson. But, if it really is a consequence of the positions of "Anscombe, Foot, Hudson, Searle, and MacIntyre" (p. 387), that we cannot properly distinguish between an equality of rights and an equality of talents, and that the obvious fallacies of deducing either directly from the other alone are not fallacies, then this consequence must by itself constitute sufficient refutation of those positions.

(b) There is no doubt what Rex said, and no reason to believe that he really meant to say anything different. But there is something different which another person might well want to assert. It is that when anyone says something he may at the same time by saying this also be doing something else. Suppose that a psychometrician is administering I.Q. tests as part of some selection operation. Suppose too that the minimum rating required by the organisation for acceptance as a whatever-it-is is 120. Then, when our psychometrician reports that a person scores – say – 100 or 130, although the proposition which the former utters certainly does not entail that anyone ought to be treated either in this way or in that, still the psychometrician's making this report equally certainly does play its part in ensuring that its subject is in fact treated thus and thus. It is true that scientific discoveries and technical skills are both used and misused, and that such speech acts as those of our imaginary psychometrician do have consequences about which both the scientists themselves and others ought to be benevolently concerned.

Certainly too the philosophical distinction just made, between the content of the proposition uttered, and what may be done by uttering it, is important. It needs to be refined and elaborated, not impatiently collapsed. (Compare Austin: 3, passim.) But it is ridiculous to take the recognition of this distinction as a reason to dismiss all attention to the distinctions between *ought* and *is* as being – in the disrespectful words of one correspondent in the *Times Higher Education Supplement*! – "unrealistic philosophizing" (*T.H.E.S.*, 18 May 1973).

In the first place we should notice that doing something by saying something often presupposes an understanding of the content of what is said. You could, for instance, scarcely insult someone by saying something which neither of you understood. So it must be absurd to dismiss all questions about the meanings and implications of scientific propositions in favour of an investigation into what scientists may or may not be doing by asserting these propositions. Then, second, we cannot possibly accept any general suggestion that scientists ought never to do or to publish any work which might be misused or misinterpreted. For that would rule out doing or publishing any work of any possible human interest, and perhaps any work at all. More particularly, we should also notice that the making of a ferocious uproar against 'Jensen and Jensenism' may well have effects quite contrary to the intentions of his enemies. For there are surely some who will in their crossgrained way bethink them that 'the lady doth protest too much', and that the very ferocity of the protests indicates a fear that uninhibited investigation would reveal that there actually are significant, genetically determined, average differences in talents or temperaments or inclinations as between some different racial groups. Suppose that someone does believe this, whether rightly or wrongly, and for whatever reason. Then the philosophising which demonstrates that such factual differences would not in any case support claims to any corresponding inequality of rights must be, not "unrealistic" but rather – if these modish words may be applied to anything not politically Radical – relevant and concerned.

(iii) Another crucial distinction is that between individuals and groups. That I belong to some group which as a group is on average less this or more that than another group to which you belong, carries no implication that I as an individual am less this or more that than you. If there are "fallacies of racism" then, as I suggested in Chapter 4, another prime specimen must be that of arguing from average characteristics of a racial group directly to conclusions about its individual members. However much we may sympathise with the correspondent who told Jensen that "If the group is to be labelled intellectually inferior, I, as a member of that group, am also inevitably and automatically labelled" (Jensen, p. 14), his argument is as an argument paradigmatically fallacious.

Suppose that this further fallacy of racism is then compounded with the other of assuming that moral equality – equality of rights and duties – necessarily presupposes a natural equality of talents. Then you are indeed forced to choose: either you accept the immoral doctrine that we ought to discriminate between individuals on the basis of their racial affiliations; or you insist that there are no genetically determined differences between racial groups in respect of talents, or temperaments or inclinations.

In the previous subsection I suggested that those who reject that immoral doctrine are imprudent to despise the modest measure of philosophical enlightenment which consists in seeing and saying these two "fallacies of racism" are indeed fallacies. I shall in the next subsection reinforce this suggestion by deploying some general and untechnical considerations making it quite likely that "the would-be factual belief" will turn out to be true: Bodmer is simply wrong to assert that "there are no *a priori* reasons for thinking" this (p. 81: his italics).

It would, I repeat, be a very bad thing if the evidence for some such conclusion were to become too strong to be either hushed up or howled down, and if that conclusion were then to be mistaken to be proof of the morality of racism, in the narrower sense just now explained. It is, therefore, not merely logically fallacious but also practically dangerous thus to tie the moral commitment to a precarious contention of fact. (Compare the parallel case of teaching the young that morality logically presupposes, and would make no sense without, a God to prescribe and to enforce its norms; which is, in a secular age, to invite them to abandon morality too if and when they grow up to lose their belief in God.)

These "fallacies of racism" raise an awkward personal challenge for the contributors to *Race, Culture and Intelligence*. For, for the reasons given, it is clearly important that their fallaciousness should be appreciated as widely as possible. Yet, once it is grasped, it also becomes obvious that the chief present targets are not racists at all. Certainly Jensen himself, Herrnstein and Eysenck – and for all I know Shockley too – have most explicitly and emphatically stated both that these fallacies are fallacies, and that they themselves utterly eschew the immoral doctrine. It is a case of "Othello's occupation's gone". So, at least until and unless they become able and willing to think more coolly and more clearly about race and racism, the best service our Penguin Educationalists could offer to the cause is that once requested by Prime Minister Attlee of Harold Laski, the then Chairman of the Labour Party Executive. A characteristically terse Attlee note recommended, simply, "a period of silence".

(iv) A second suggestion on why Jensen's conclusion should be thought to matter so much can be found in the second passage

quoted from Rex. While ready reluctantly to admit "that there is
. . . a genetic component in measured intelligence", what he
cannot allow is that there are any differences "so great that
manipulation of the environment is not capable of fundamentally altering them". The campaign against Jensenism is thus to be
seen, like Lysenko's murderous battle against Vavilov, as part of
a great war between environmentalists and hereditarians.[15] The
reason why it is thought to be progressive to emphasise
environment rather than heredity is that the former is believed
to be always more immediately and more effectively manipul-
able than the latter.

This is a mistake. The division between what can and cannot
be remedied by human action does not follow the same line as
that between what is and is not determined by heredity. What
can or cannot be remedied depends, of course, upon who and
when and where you are. But it is already possible to point to
genetically determined defects which can be offset by the
application of presently available knowledge: "a child who has
inherited the genes for PKV ["a recessive genetic defect of
metabolism which results in brain damage"] can grow up
normally if his diet is controlled to eliminate certain proteins
which contain phenylalanine" (Jensen, p. 120). On the other
side there are all manner of defects, which no one believes to be
genetically determined and which, nearly sixty years after
Lenin's October coup, the most absolute and least scrupulous of
governments has been unable to remove. (Compare Jencks,
p. 64.)

To bring out that this simple assumption about manipulability
is wrong, and for other reasons too, consider now a rather
abstract argument to show how unlikely it is that the distribution
of genes determining the relevant kinds of ability is the same in
the gene pools of all races, and of all geographical and other
sub-groups within those races. First, absolutely no one denies
that the defining characteristics of races are hereditarily
determined. Next, almost no one denies that abilities are also to
some considerable but not precisely known extent hereditarily
determined. So it ought to be obvious that, unless Providence
has been taking a hand to ensure that at least in this respect
things are as Penguin Educationalists would wish them to be,
there *may* be statistically significant correlations between the two.
Certainly no one has any business to rule the idea out a priori.

Suppose, however, that at some particular time – say, if you like, in 4004 B.C. – Providence did provide the desired perfectly even distribution yet rashly permitted environmental factors to operate as usual. We should have then to expect a Fall from that original equilibrium. For environmentally determined differences in patterns of mating choice and in reproductive performance, some of these differences no doubt attributable to authentically racist attitudes and policies, would surely by the hypothesis be working to produce changes in the gene pools of the various races and of subgroups within those races.

A process of this kind is probably occurring now in the United States. For black middle- and upper-class families have fewer children than their white counterparts, while black lower-class families have more than their white opposite numbers. (See, for instance, D. P. Moynihan 'Employment, Income and the Ordeal of the Negro Family' in Parsons and Clark.) So, assuming that ability is at least partly determined by the genes, and that relevant hereditary ability correlates positively with elevation on the scale of social class, we presumably must infer that the gene pool of the black Americans is in this respect, and at this time, in comparison with the gene pool of the white Americans, deteriorating. The first premise of this syllogism is the second scarcely questionable assumption of the whole argument. The second premise is more contested, if not more contestable. But not only is there abundant evidence that it is true wherever promotion is desired and wherever there is some measure of equality of opportunity – wherever, that is, we really are speaking of social class and not caste. It is also obvious that, on these assumptions, and given always that we are here talking only about whatever abilities are relevant to this particular sort of success, it must be true.

What is neither obvious nor in fact true is that the same positive correlations between social class standing and relevant hereditary ability which obtain for the parents will obtain for the children also. For here we have to take account of the phenomenon of regression to the mean. This is both very important and too rarely noticed: bright parents tend on average to have bright children, but, again on average, not so bright as themselves; whereas dull parents tend on average to have dull children but, again on average, not so dull as themselves. It is this fact which guarantees that approach to the ideal of perfect equality of opportunity will not be approach to the realisation of a *Brave New World*; the nightmare of a totally immobile society in which the children and the grandchildren of the alphas will all be alphas in their turn, while the children and the grandchildren of the deltas and epsilons are all like their forebears deltas and epsilons. (See, for instance, Eysenck in *New Society*, 25 October 1973; and compare Jencks, p. 81.)

The process of relative genetic decline, supposing that it is indeed occurring, is certainly one which, given the political will and adequate research, could be checked and reversed.[16] So it is paradoxical, and much worse, that a muddle-headed and obscurantist refusal to recognise the live possibility that there are such differences in the present genetic endowment of different racial groups, and an equally muddle-headed and doctrinaire insistence that genetic factors cannot be important because if they were they would be beyond the range of environmental manipulation, should be getting in the way of the research to discover what is happening and how things might be improved. I quote again from the execrated heresiarch: "The possible consequences of our failure seriously to study these questions may well be viewed by future generations as our society's greatest injustice to Negro Americans" (Jensen, pp. 178-9).

3.   *Nevertheless the Facts Do Matter*

Although it was necessary to indicate reasons why there may well be genetically determined interracial differences of a kind which many today most categorically deny, this chapter must end, where it began, with education rather than with eugenics. In Subsection 2 (ii) I asked why it is thought to matter so much whether there are such differences, and proceeded to argue that the answer to the question whether there in fact are cannot by itself either justify or refute any normatively racist conclusions. But this is not to show that there is no point in finding out the facts. There is.

The point is paradoxical. If no one at all was interested in what racial group they or anyone else belonged to, then the questions would indeed be trifling or at most of purely theoretical interest. All that would matter for any practical purpose would be the hereditary endowments and limitations of each individual. To the educator these would of course matter as the determinants of the ultimate, and we hope very wide limits of the educational possibilities for that individual. Since in that happier world there would by the hypothesis be no racially assortative mating, all racial group differences of all kinds would in any case presumably tend to disappear.

But in fact we live in this world. Since most people, however regrettably, actually are interested in what racial groups they and some others belong to, mating choices are in part determined by racial as well as other kinds of affinity. This fact, as we have just seen, may tend to produce and consolidate other differences between some racial groups. Another more particular manifestation of the same general fact is that people build assumptions about races and racial groups into their political, social and educational policies. Notoriously these assumptions have sometimes been of hereditary differences which certainly do not obtain: that no black is capable of becoming a Nobel Prize scientist; that all members of the putative Jewish race have an inherited tendency monstrously to exploit; and so on. But, so long as any would-be factual assumptions about races and racial groups are built into any policies, it will remain practically important to discover whether such assumptions are true. A large part of what we have natural and social scientists for is to enable us to get the facts right when we debate and decide policies.

The particular racial assumption which now guides much public policy in the United States is precisely the one which Jensen is so abused for questioning. Thus in 1965 the Department of Labour boldly proclaimed: "Intelligence potential is distributed among Negro infants in the same proportion and pattern as among Icelanders or Chinese, or any other group. ... There is absolutely no question of any genetic differential." His work is, therefore, a paradigm of practically relevant and socially concerned research: "it was", as he says, "part of my personal philosophy that a scientist should try to bring his technical expertise to bear on practical as well as theoretical problems" (p. 5).

Some of the educational consequences of what seems to be a false assumption are described by Eysenck in 'The Dangers in a New Orthodoxy' (*New Humanist,* July 1973). In Berkeley in California I.Q. tests were stopped because they had shown that the percentage of Educationally Sub Normal (E.S.N.) black children was greater than the percentage of E.S.N. children in the total school population. The surplus to quota E.S.N. black children were then removed from the E.S.N. class and put into an ordinary class. In the interests of the certainly false doctrine that equality of rights presupposes and validates equality of talents, a lot of children who desperately needed all the specialist educational help which they could get were deprived of that help; and put instead into a class where they forthwith – very understandably – disrupted the teaching and learning of others. Similarly misguided policies were followed for the same reason and with similar results at the other end of the I.Q. scale. The upshot was general exasperation and discontent among both black and white children and parents; with the black demanding, and getting, a separate 'Black House' school unit (compare Eysenck, p. 23). The rejection of racism thus led – by, it seems, factual mistake out of logical fallacy – to a classic case of racism: educational selection and segregation on racial grounds.

Again, the Department of Health, Education and Welfare, misguided by the same assumption, insists that any disproportionate representation of any racial in any social group can only be the immediate or ultimate outcome of immoral racial discrimination. It further urges that such situations should be rectified by 'affirmative action'; which, being translated, is racial discrimination in favour of members of underrepresented racial groups. Once again the rejection of the immoral doctrine of racism, confounded by various intellectual deficiencies, leads back to racism; and, of course, in so far as 'affirmative action' does really in practice amount to more than an innocuous preference – all-other-things-being-equal, it must result in a lowering of standards in education – and in every other sphere to which it is applied. Symbolic of that lowering is an advertisement which I collected for my *Philosophical Scrapbook* during the academic year 1970/1. It contrives to be at the same time both racist and self-contradictory: "The University of Michigan", candidates are assured, "is a non-discriminatory affirmative action employer."

Part Two

6   Teaching and Testing

Part One examined various misunderstandings of the presuppositions and of the actual or possible discoveries of certain human sciences, and argued that most of these misunderstandings are a threat not only to the defence of educational standards but also to the pursuit of these sciences themselves. Now in Part Two we pass on to ideas which belong primarily within education. The *Times Higher Education Supplement* introduced a contribution in 1972 with the blurb: "Laurence Lerner says that he is tired of accusations that the university imposes assessment to provide labour-fodder for capitalism, and offers students a solution." What is proposed as a solution is that at some late stage "each student would be asked if he wishes to be assessed. If he says 'No' he will continue his courses as usual, and may well do better work than otherwise, since they will have his full attention. . . . A student who elected not to be assessed would not get a degree, and much thought would have to be given to what document he did get. It is essential that no stigma be attached to such a document. It must be carefully distinguished from failing one's degree, and it should never be awarded as a compensation to those who do in fact fail" (*T.H.E.S.*, 27 October 1972).

1.   *A Certificate of No Known Achievement*

The main purpose of the present chapter is to challenge the assumption – apparently shared by both Lerner, a Professor of English in the University of Sussex, and those students for whom this proposal is intended to cater – that assessment is related to the business of teaching and learning, if it is related at all, only contingently; so that "a student [who] says 'No' [to assessment] will continue his courses as usual, and may well do better work than otherwise, since they will have his full attention".[17]

(i) Before proceeding to this main and philosophical business there are two other fashionable assumptions to dispose of.

(a) The first is that academic assessment, and in particular perhaps the use of written examinations, is peculiarly related to a capitalist system. Like many others Lerner is "tired of hearing the university accused of acting as society's lackey, imposing on students an assessment process they hate for the sake of providing labour-fodder for capitalism". Well may we all be tired. For, as "the implacable Professor" once said, "there is nothing so plain boring as the constant repetition of statements which are not true, and sometimes not even faintly sensible; if we can reduce this a bit it will be all to the good" (Austin: 2, p. 5).

Lerner, however, sets about the good work of reduction too half-heartedly. He says: "I am tired of it because it is an absurd oversimplification; but in so far as it is true, it ought to be recognised that graduates enter the world of capitalism because they decide to." This misses the point. For what is reiterated so tediously is a complete irrelevance, not an oversimplification. Capitalism has nothing to do with it at all: and in fact no one seriously tries to show that it does. Do any of the students whom Lerner has in mind ever bother to deny the familiar facts: that in Britain, for instance, the nationalised industries are no less and no more concerned than those not yet nationalised to discover whether candidates for employment have got a degree, and how good a degree; or that this concern is as strong or stronger in employers outside commerce and industry, particularly in education? Or does anyone who says this sort of thing nowadays attempt either to discover or to deny the perhaps slightly less familiar fact that the emphasis upon examinations and upon formal academic qualifications is if anything heavier in the fully socialist countries of the Soviet Bloc? (See, for instance, the article mentioned in Note 8.)

Charity compels us to attribute such widespread failures even to attempt the most obviously relevant comparisons in part to simple silliness. But realism requires that we also recognise a large element of sheer bad faith. This remarkable failure is then to be interpreted as a sign: either that a concern about assessment is being more or less disingenuously exploited in what may or may not be someone else's campaign against capitalism; or that an understandable, if not perhaps very noble, distaste for the demands of life and work outside the cloisters is being misrepresented in the more admired guise of social and socialist commitment.

Compare and contemplate two similarly twisted perform- ances: first, of those for whom industrial pollution and the destruction of species are a peculiarly or even exclusively capitalist ill; and, second, of those Radical criminologists who still go on suggesting, or even asserting, that the evils of crime and punishment are a mainly or wholly pre-socialist pheno- menon. When the former simply ignore, for instance, the contrast, which I myself experienced in 1965 and 1966, between the (by then) astonishingly clean air of Pittsburgh and the pollution of medieval Cracow downwind from the Lenin Steel Mills of Nowy Huta, it becomes hard to concede that their concerns are primarily environmental or conservationist. When the latter take absolutely no account of the realities of *The Gulag Archipelago*, it is plain impossible to pretend that theirs is a straightforward and unqualified hostility to the evils of imprisonment and other penal sanctions. For it is precisely the first revolutionary socialist country which has had, surely, a larger proportion of its population in worse prisons than any other? Bad faith of this kind is inimical, both to the balanced appraisal of the claims of rival social systems, and to the diagnosis and cure of actual or alleged social evils.

(b) The second assumption to be challenged is one of the background conditions of Lerner's argument. Throughout he takes it that the only interests to be considered are those of the teacher and the student. Thus he writes: "We can ask who benefits from the whole thing, and who therefore should be responsible for initiating it. Obviously the beneficiary of the teaching is the student. But is it not also the student who is the beneficiary of assessment? If he is not tested, he will not know how good he is. If he is not stimulated by impending assessment he may not work." Lerner then adds a comment: "Clearly, members of a faculty have a direct interest in the second of these. It should be the right of any faculty member to refuse to teach a student who is not working." Selfishly, yet not only selfishly, I wish that this last point were as obvious to everyone as it is to Lerner.

Certainly it can be salutary to say that the prime direct beneficiary in teaching and learning, and in the assessment of achievement in learning, is the student. But then we must remember that our inference is warranted only where the word 'student' is applied to a person who is as such committed to learning. We are not entitled to draw the same conclusion where the word is employed, as in fact it often is, simply to pick out members of a certain socio-economic group. For a person may enjoy, and hence wish to retain, that status without having any inclination or commitment to study: just as a person may enjoy, and hence wish to retain, the status and emoluments of a teacher without having any inclination or commitment to teaching. If someone is a student only in this purely socio-economic sense, then that status provides no ground for inferring that he would himself benefit from appropriate academic assessment.

Yet once these things have been said, we have also to remember that there is a big external world beyond the walls of the university. This wider world, which in one way or another sustains and supports the entire operation, has some legitimate interests in, and some proper claims over, what is or is not done inside. We need not in this chapter plunge into a general discussion of questions of academic freedom and academic responsibility, although I shall have something to say about these later. For present purposes it is enough simply to state that, although the external world should in our special case waive many of the usual payer's rights to call the tunes, even the most liberal benefactors may reasonably require some guarantees, both that piping is actually going on, and that it is being done as well as may be.

In particular we should remember in the present context, as Lerner it seems does not, that in Britain today all university and polytechnic students other than those whose parents are committing enviably, and therefore unacceptably, higher incomes are financed from public funds. It should surely be seen as odd and anomalous that a substantial proportion of our young citizens are thus temporary state pensioners as soon as, or even sooner than, they come legally of age; and before their ordinary working lives have begun. Certainly anyone who, like Lerner, wants to reduce still further the already pretty modest demands which the typical British university department makes on its students, ought to link their recommendations with some proposal for the loan financing of the maintenance of the students in these institutions – the loans presumably to be repaid by a surcharge on the income tax, if any, on the future income of these students. (Such proposals could, by the way, have the incidental merit of removing the scandalous requirement that the higher-income parents of those in tertiary education must support their adult offspring.)

Lerner, however, gives no indication that he recognises even the most modest of outside claims. His proposal specifically provides that for his examination dropouts there is to be no assessment of quality, while the requirement that they should do any work at all appears primarily as a matter of maintaining "the right of any faculty member to refuse to teach a student who is not working". Thus, in describing his proposed certificate of the award of a not-degree – a document to which "It is essential that no stigma be attached" – Lerner writes: "It would presumably state that the student had attended the university for three years, and there is a problem here: for to say someone has attended the university means that he has done his share of the work, not simply sat in the sun, so that there would have to be some check on his progress. But it should simply be a check on whether he has worked, and has cooperated with his teachers, with no reference to the quality of his work; and one imagines that the check need not be too rigorous."

Certainly no one acquainted with the generality of academics, and in particular with those most eager to think up new concessions to offer in hopes of appeasing our present student discontented, would expect any such checks to be rigorous; in a purely descriptive sense of the word 'expect'. But it is not equally obvious why it is imagined that they ought not to be, and why we may not expect them to be, very rigorous indeed, in a purely normative sense.

This distinction between two senses of 'expect' is generally important (Flew: 7). But it is perhaps especially relevant in education. It is one thing to expect someone to act in such and such a way, where this involves only an entirely neutral and detached prediction. It is quite another to expect someone to do something, where this is a matter of your committing yourself on how they ought to act. One very common fallacy is to dismiss a claim of the second kind by asking, in the first sense and therefore irrelevantly: 'What did you expect?' Lord Nelson's famous signal before Trafalgar exploited the same ambiguity; and the great victory which followed surely provides in some measure an instance of what, in Chapter 2, I labelled the

England Expects Effect. Wise parents and wise teachers will continue to take advantage of the same ambiguity in order to encourage similar if less glorious endeavours.

(ii) It is not clear why Lerner thinks: that "to say someone has attended the university means that he has done his share of the work"; or that "It is essential that no stigma be attached to such a document." In the first case the initial point is a matter of correct language. For the expression "attended the university" is one which a fastidious referee might well choose to employ when he wished, in both honesty and charity, neither to say nor to imply that his subject had done any academic work or made any academic progress. At a deeper level this insensitivity to verbal niceties can be seen as symptomatic of the ambivalence of Lerner's project. Since the perverse object of the whole exercise is to provide a worthwhile certificate of no proved achievement, there is a certain looking-glass logic in his thus wanting to construe mere attendance as necessarily involving something more, and then going on backwards to indicate that that more need be so little that no one who wanted to meet his "not . . . too rigorous" requirements could fail to satisfy them.

(a) Next, apparently, "It is essential that no stigma be attached to such a document." Lerner just tells us this, giving no reasons. Presumably he takes it to be obvious that no one must ever be allowed to feel inferior; even, or perhaps especially, where they are. In his next sentence Lerner says of the new certificate: "It must be carefully distinguished from failing one's degree, and it should never be awarded as a compensation to those who do in fact fail." Now certainly there is a difference between he who has loved and lost and he who has never loved at all, and any records should no doubt make this distinction clear. But there are also differences, which to his credit Lerner also insists must be kept clear in the records, between both of these and he who has loved and won.

The absurdity arises when Lerner assumes as something plumb obvious that it is possible, and indeed essential, that a certificate of no proved achievement shall be no less valuable than a certificate of tested and proved achievement. This could only be where, and in so far as, no one cares positively about the difference between the two. Yet Lerner himself obviously does so care. For he remains enough of a traditionalist to want to provide: both for the maintainance of the old order – assessing, and recording the assessment of, performance; and for the introduction of this carefully distinguished new form of certification – a form specifically not requiring or recording any level of actual tested achievement. Lerner is, therefore, ambivalent: as between, on the one hand, his old-fashioned interest in academic merit and the proof of it; and, on the other hand, his proposed concessions to the demands of student militancy and the new egalitarianism.

Anyone who like Lerner demands that the qualities of performances should sometimes be assessed has got to come to terms with the truth that any kind of merit must be, albeit presumptively and defeasibly, a cut above the lack of that form of merit; and hence that any form of proved merit must be, with the same qualifications, a cut above the lack of that form of proved merit. So, for instance, so long as it is allowed that it is a good thing to have achieved a certain degree of mastery of Canadian geography, a certificate recording that under test you have in fact shown that degree of mastery is, all other things being equal, bound to be more valuable than one testifying only that – in some "not . . . too rigorous" sense of 'attend' – you have attended courses on that subject.

(b) It should go without saying, although in these days it had better be said, that all this is entirely consistent with a recognition that academic achievements are not the only or the most valuable varieties of human excellence. Everyone who has taught even one or two generations of students will be able to recall splendid individuals whose two twos or thirds represented great personal achievements; as well as some others much less splendid who contrived to combine the winning of the highest academic honours with every kind of nastiness of character. And one of those opting for the certificate of attendance might – just might – be a future Einstein. And so on. But all this leaves the basic theoretical point untouched.

(c) The new egalitarianism mentioned a moment ago has to be distinguished from other, older, and less educationally subversive species. It is by definition, and might indeed be better labelled as, egalitarianism of outcome. The concern is to minimise all differences in talents or application, in achievement or reward. For the new egalitarian 'competition' is in any context a very bad word. But education is of special interest to him. This is one of the areas in which people are most likely to be seen to differ in abilities and – if given the chance – in application and achievement also. So he is especially eager here to prevent any tests which reveal such differences, and perhaps even encourage and increase them. Failing that, he is eager to prevent the publication of the results of whatever tests may nevertheless be made.

The basic ideological drive of the new egalitarian is in this reinforced by two independent forces: first, a general awareness – often in fact an exaggerated over-awareness – of the fallibility of all human test procedures; and, second, the unmentionable interests of the least efficient and least devoted teachers. Anyone who has ever attended study conferences on assessment methods will remember that there is always someone who at some stage urges that the moral of all these difficulties and lapses from the ideal is that we should abandon the whole weary struggle for improvement. As for the second force it is necessary, and at present sufficient, to say only two things – both with reference to a proposal traditionally popular in the National Union of Teachers (N.U.T.).

The proposal is that all external examinations should be abolished in favour of personal reports on pupils by their teachers. First, we should never forget the reasons why the party of progress in the last century fought and eventually won a long struggle to recruit the Civil Service by public competitive examinations rather than through private personal recommendations. It was because only in this way could the recruiters hope to discover the relative merits of candidates coming from all over the country; and, incidentally, the relative merits of their different schools and the value of any personal recommendations from their teachers. Nor, second, should we ever forget that the performance of our pupils in public examinations provides the most generally reliable index of how well we ourselves have been teaching. It is, therefore, to be expected (descriptive) that those who are not confident of their own showing on such tests will be keen to see the last of the tests themselves. It is also to be expected (descriptive) that a union which is industrial as opposed to craft will – as the N.U.T. in fact does – go for flat-rate wage increases right across the board, and the fewer questions about application or skill the better.

The new egalitarianism of outcome is totally different from the older ideal of equality of opportunity. To believe in "la carrière ouverte aux talents" – one of the principles of 1789 – is by no means to assume that everyone does in fact have equal abilities, or that everyone will in fact, if given an equal chance, employ whatever abilities they do have with equal energy and determination. Nor, certainly, is it to be committed to minimising differences in achievement or in reward. Indeed this ideal of equality of opportunity would lose much of its point if our natural endowments were more or less equal; or if the extrinsic rewards to be expected from the different degrees of application of different talents were – or are – going in any case to be made very much the same.

Both these two ideals should also be distinguished from the "a man's a man for all that" egalitarianism expressed by Captain Rainborough in the Putney debates of our own New Model Army: "And I do believe that the poorest he that is in England hath a life to live, as much as the greatest he." This has a lot to do with one man one vote, and with that old-time political democracy which essentially involves that we can "vote the scoundrels out". It surely also has some connection with, although it could scarcely be said to entail, equality of opportunity. But both are obviously very far removed from the new egalitarianism of outcome.

(d) From this somewhat discursive description of that ideal we return to Lerner. Had the suggestion "that no stigma be attached to such a document" come from a wholehearted protagonist of this standpoint there would have been no inconsistency between particular proposal and general ideological stance. For as a new egalitarian he would necessarily be dedicated to devaluing, wherever he could not deny, all differences of talents or application, of achievement or reward. But Lerner is not a new egalitarian. He cares about academic achievement; and, consequently, he wants to know about it. For him and his like – for our like – his new certificate of mere attendance cannot but, at least so long as it can be compared with a traditional degree document, have a stigma attached to it. His proposal is thus, at this point, incoherent.

The new egalitarian, on the other hand, will have no difficulty in thinking kindly of a certificate of no known achievement. Yet he still has to reject Lerner's compromise. For so long as we continue to allow others to get old-style merit degrees, with their obnoxious references to tested achievement, there are bound to be discernible and discerned inequalities between those whose levels are in fact different; and that, of course, will never do. So the new egalitarian will be best advised to press, as he surely will, for the complete abolition of all grading as odiously discriminatory. Part of the price of this reckless programme will be revealed in Section 2 below.

2.   *Sincerity of Purpose and the Monitoring of Progress*

Now at last we have come to our central question: 'How far would Lerner's proposed concessions be compatible with the idea of a university as a place of teaching and learning?' These basic notions are curiously but significantly muffled in Lerner's account of the qualifications required for the certificate of no known achievement. He says of his assessment dropout: "there would have to be some check on his progress . . . it should simply be a check on whether he has worked, and has cooperated with his teachers, with no reference to the quality of his work. . . ."

Wait a minute: 'Progress in what?'; 'What work?'; and 'Cooperation in what?' It would presumably not be relevant to establish that candidates had been working to raise their Kinsey ratings, and that they had made good progress in fulfilling this agreeable albeit strictly extra-curricular aim. I hope that it would still not be accepted as relevant – even in the more Red Base departments – that they had been cooperative with teachers in their political activities. The work surely has to be the work of learning whatever it is that our student is supposed to be learning, the progress has to be progress in that work, and the cooperation has to be with teachers as teachers. While I was first writing about Lerner the largest recruit to the Liberal bench in the House of Commons, Cyril Smith, was being quoted in the press as saying: "There should be no Government grants for student agitators who do not work at their desks."

(i) Although almost all the Education Correspondents were predictably scandalised by this breath of fresh Lancashire air, it is hard to see any justification – so long as the crux was, as it surely was, not the agitation but that they "do not work at their desks". This at last gets the emphasis on the objects of the whole exercise and, consequently, on the key terms 'learning' and 'teaching'. Although both do have non-intentional employments, they are primarily used to describe intentional ongoings.

To be engaged in learning is thus to be trying to master some piece of possible knowledge – whether knowledge of how to do something or knowledge that such and such is the case. To be engaged in teaching someone else is to be engaged in trying to bring it about that that person masters some item of possible knowledge. In both cases there has to be an object, or perhaps one should say a subject – something to be learnt or taught. The once popular slogan 'We teach children, not subjects' makes nonsense if it is construed – as the French would say if only they spoke English – at the foot of the letter (Scheffler, pp. 38 ff.).

It is the intentionality which carries the crucial implications. For no one can truly be said to be acting from some intention unless his actions display at least some minimal consistency with that intention: "It is", as Kai Lung says in one of Ernest Bramah's tales of old China, "a mark of insincerity of purpose to seek the sacred Emperor in low-class teashops."

It is, further, a necessary condition for my sincerity in any purpose that I should be concerned whether, how far, and how well, I am succeeding, or have succeeded, in that purpose. To be indifferent as to whether or not this is indeed the sacred Emperor is as much a mark of insincerity as it is to set about my pretended purpose of seeking him in a fashion calculated to ensure its frustration. If, therefore, anyone is a genuine learner trying to master some piece of possible knowledge, or an authentic teacher trying to bring it about that someone else masters such an item of possible knowledge; then, necessarily, they must be concerned whether, how far, and how well they are succeeding. But they can scarcely claim to be thus concerned if they take no steps to discover the answers to those questions. And the most general word for all such attempts is – spare the mark – 'assessment'. For any genuine teacher, therefore, and for any genuine learner too, the contention that there ought to be no assessment and no examinations of any kind must be a paradigm case of the properly non-negotiable demand.

(ii) Once this main point has been put we must notice how much and how little is at stake, and what sort of thesis it is.

(a) What is ruled out is every suggestion of any systematic education freed of all assessment and examination. Lerner says: "a student [who] says 'No' [to assessment] will continue his courses as usual, and may well do better work than otherwise, since they will have his full attention". To this my more fundamental objection is: not that the not-too-distant prospect of final examinations, like the threat of execution in the morning, concentrates the mind marvellously; but that the notions of pursuing a course of instruction and of trying to master its contents, without any kind of assessment at all, are simply self-contradictory.

In recent years, particularly in North America, some people employed as teachers have discovered conscientious objections to all grading, and have in consequence refused to return any reports on the quality of the work done by those entrusted to their charge. While I was in Calgary one of these sent a manifesto to this effect to the President of the University of Alberta. Obviously this ought to have been received, politely and perhaps with regret, as a letter of resignation. Certainly it should be anyone's right to maintain this objection, if they must: and, in so far as it is a principled and disinterested conviction, open to revision or withdrawal in deference to good reasons given, it deserves respect as such. But to allow this is a very different thing from allowing any rights to employments inconsistent with this sincere conviction. If you believe that war is always morally wrong, then you cannot reasonably demand a job as a fighter pilot – notwithstanding that you are both in physique and in educational attainments eminently suitable for aircrew training. If you are a hardline Roman Catholic, then you are not being irrelevantly, and therefore improperly, discriminated against if this fact was the decisive reason why you were not hired as the gynæcologist with special responsibility for the contraception clinic. Generally, the having of principles comes cheaper in proportion to the liberalism of your society. Yet even in the most liberal, sane society they can never cost you nothing at all.

A third illustration comes again from *Race, Culture and Intelligence*: it is no doubt part of the claim of that work to constitute Penguin Education. Daniels, Head of the Further Professional Training Division in the School of Education at Nottingham, and Houghton, Head of the Division of Behavioural Sciences at Huddersfield Polytechnic, rejoice that "in these new circumstances the whole grading system, the whole system of meritocratic badges, is coming into question". But then, in the following paragraph, after condemning the suggested motives of anyone so foolish as to have mistaken them to mean what they said, they surreptitiously readmit most of what they had just now hoped to be seeing off for good: "Those, usually in the top jobs, in education and administration often defend the grading system, sarcastically asking, 'Would you approve of amateur surgery?' We are not suggesting any such thing. Surgery, in common with a large number of other high-order skills, will always require *proven* competence. But this is no argument to justify the vast body of irrelevant examination organizations at every level or the widespread use of verbal intelligence tests" (p. 73: italics theirs).

This wretched display constitutes an excellent textbook example of something mentioned earlier, in Subsubsection 1 (ii)(c): the tendency to shift unwittingly to and fro between outright rejection of all assessment and all examinations, and a less ruinous objection either to particular kinds of examination or to any assessment of what you consider to be the wrong sorts of work. Tests of "*proven competence*" in surgery, or in any other low or "high-order skills", are entirely indiscernible from theoretical and practical examinations: under the revolutionary new Daniels and Houghton regime there are to be no gifts, only donations!

Furthermore, what are these "irrelevant examination organizations" supposed to be irrelevant to? Surely it is not that they are thought to be setting examinations which do not relate either to their published syllabi or to the courses pursued by their examinees? If, more likely, it is these syllabi and these courses which are being condemned as irrelevant to some other here unstated objective; then this condemnation – however justifiable it might be in the right place – is itself irrelevant. For it is no objection to assessment or examination as such – to "the whole grading system, the whole system of meritocratic badges" – that these happen sometimes to be employed within or with reference to courses which would be much better not pursued at all.

(b) What has been shown is that assessment and examination in some form are essential to systematic education as such. But this is not, of course, to provide: either wholesale justification for all presently established methods and practices; or particular justification for one favoured method against all possible rivals. There remains vast scope for research, discussion, even negotiation about what methods of assessment and examination are in fact most helpful and least distracting to the advancement of what learning. So far as my own main thesis goes there remains room for argument as to whether it is necessary to have actual degree certificates recording levels of achievement, or to publish degree results and/or course grades, or to make transcripts of course grade record cards available to potential employers.

What does limit the area for sensible discussion of this second cluster of questions is not any philosophical thesis but the practical fact that it quite obviously is necessary to have and to use such attested records of learning achievement in all those cases – which are certainly not all cases – where the subject of that learning and the nature of that achievement are such as to constitute a positively valuable qualification. We can then go on to debate in detail what is a proper, or a good, or an essential qualification for what. Maybe we shall discover that there are some whole departments which provide only what ought to be seen not as a qualification for something but as a disqualification for anything!

Although I have indicated in passing one or two of the reasons why I believe that to abandon external examinations would precipitate a spiralling educational decline, these particular reasons, and most of the others, are not in any usefully strong sense philosophical.[18] But it is just worth pointing out that one of our able young philosophers of education might well develop a powerful new argument for this conservative conclusion, drawing materials from the later Wittgenstein. For the main burden of the *Philosophical Investigations* is that having rules and standards in general, and having language in particular, are essentially social matters; and that no one could have, and know that he had, any rules, standards or language in complete isolation from all other people. (Having said this, and remembering *Knowledge and Control,* I must now emphasise that to say this is not, of course, to say that the distinctions we are thus enabled to make either cannot correspond, or cannot be known to correspond, to any objective differences 'without the mind'.) The judgements of the individual teachers, never to be checked and tested against anything more public and more objective, are perhaps tantamount to no standards at all. (See Jones (ed.); and, of course, compare Wittgenstein himself.)

(c) The main argument in the present Section 2 is one of several which in various spheres insist upon a logically necessary

connection between sincerity of purpose and readiness to
monitor progress, or the lack of it. Think for a moment of Karl
Popper; who surely of all the substantial philosophers of our
century is the one whose characteristic philosophical ideas are
most, and most widely, relevant for those who are not specialist
students of the subject. One unifying principle running through
the whole of Popper's work is the crucial importance of learning
from our mistakes, whether in natural and social science, or in
political and social affairs.[19] Thus, in his view, the essence of
heroic science is to form bold, clear theories; and then to labour
to find or to produce situations in which, if these theories are
false, they can be shown to be. The nerve of the difference
between true science and such degenerate or pseudo-sciences as
astrology, psychoanalysis and twentieth-century post-Marx
Marxism, is that theories of the latter kind are by all manner of
immunising strategems made unfalsifiable by anything which
either does or conceivably might occur. Since any exploration of
fact must explain why things happen thus and thus, *and not
otherwise*, such unfalsifiability can be purchased only at the price
of losing all true explanatory power.

So also in his social philosophy, Popper insists on piecemeal,
reformist policies, subject to constant critical review. He utterly
rejects wholesale, utopian social engineering. He rejects it
precisely because policies of total transformation cannot be –
and are not intended to be – halted, altered, or reversed in the
light of appraisals of results actually achieved. One thing which
Popper himself has not stressed, but which I want to make much
of now, is that these are matters not of rationality only but of
good faith too. If it really is the true explanation which I am
after, not the all-out defence of my own treasured theory, then I
must be ready to test that theory to destruction; and to seek a
better if it fails. Where, and to the extent that, I either avert my
gaze from evidence which threatens to disprove some favourite
belief or – still worse – bigotedly persist in it in defiance of
disproof; there, and to that extent, I reveal that my professions
of desire to discover and to know the truth are not sincere.

If you really are pressing your political or social policy as a
means to further human goods, then you must be ready, even
eager, to monitor the actual success or failure of that policy in
achieving those stated ends; and ready, even eager, to abandon
it when, and in so far as, critical appraisal shows it not to be by

this criterion a success. If, and to the extent that, you do not try to find out how well your policy is working, judged as a means to those stated ends, but instead show yourself indifferent to whether they are being realised or not; then, and to that extent, you reveal that those stated ends either never were, or have since ceased to be, your actual and sincerely pursued objectives.

3.   *Supplementary Observations on the Nature of Teaching.*

James Andris contributed a paper on 'Person X is teaching' to *Philosophy of Education 1971,* edited by R. D. Heslep: this was a predecessor of the volume in which the first version of the present chapter was published. I offer one or two additions to the foundations which Andris laid there.

(i) He was concerned, as we have been, with intentional teaching.

(a) Yet we have to query his incidental claim: "It is interesting to note that the first person sentence 'I am teaching' has no non-intentional sense" (p. 235). For the word 'teaching' is used non-intentionally in such rueful first-person sentences as 'We are (by our pill-popping habits) teaching our children to join the drug scene.'

(b) Perhaps here especially to try is not necessarily to succeed. Notice however that when this permanent possibility of failure is very much in mind we are apt to say, not that we are without prefix or suffix learning or teaching, but rather that we are trying to learn or trying to teach. It is worth one or two sentences to bring out exactly what we are doing when we do this. We are not reporting the introduction into previously non-intentional ongoings of a new element of purpose and effort. We are instead explicating and emphasising something which must already be there whenever anyone is in the present senses learning or teaching, and we are explicating and emphasising this in order to make quite sure that no one mistakes it that the learning or teaching which is going on will necessarily climax in success.

(ii) The main point which concerns us made by Andris is given as his Condition 3a for the truth of the sentence 'Person X is teaching'. Andris says: "the following rule must be among the ones being followed by X to bring about this rule-conforming behaviour: The learner's behaviour is to be corrected by X whenever it is judged by X that such correction may or will result in the desired behaviour" (p. 236: Andris notes here that he has found only one suggestion to this effect in the literature, namely Keith Sayre 'Teaching Ourselves by Learning Machines', *Journal of Philosophy,* 1970, p. 916).

(a) If this suggestion is substantially right, and I am sure that it is, then various possible candidates for the title 'teaching' will have to be ploughed. Thus, as Andris points out, a library assistant who helps a student find a book will be facilitating teaching or facilitating learning. But he will not be himself teaching. Nor will the writer of a textbook, however much he exploits his experience as a teacher in writing this book, be, as he writes, teaching.

More interestingly, the specification of this watching and correcting Condition 3a seems to carry the consequence that formal and uninterrupted lectures given without any arrangements for subsequent feedback to the lecturer, must be, as exercises in teaching, disqualified. If I give a lecture on television, then there are many things which may make this count as educational – its content, for instance, or my strong desire that that content shall be assimilated by the unseen public. But the exercise will become teaching only if and when it is backed up by some sort of Open University programme of correspondence and/or tutorials enabling me to monitor the responses and to check the misunderstandings of at least some of that audience.

Again, if Andris is right, then apparently many Professors on the continent of Europe – and perhaps on other continents too – do no teaching; although they are paid to teach, and do in fact lecture. For there are, we are told, those who – often from afar – simply come, lecture, and, without any consequent questions or discussion, go. In the meantime those whom we can scarcely call their students pursue their own bent, their progress unmonitored and unassessed by any teacher until their final examination scripts are graded; but not, of course, annotated and returned. It is, incidentally, because for good and familiar reasons this is with final examinations the almost universal practice that there can be some case, though not much, for saying that finals are pedagogically distracting and educationally irrelevant. But our only basis for saying this requires us also to insist that tests of some sort by which progress can be monitored are an essential of teaching. So too is the checking of whatever deficiencies and misunderstandings may be revealed by these tests. It simply is bad practice, and downright negligent, not to provide some form of commentary on test scripts.

Accurate grading, and the thorough and constructive annotation of written work, are exacting and often wearisome tasks. We should, therefore, suspect our own motives if we find ourselves developing what we would like to regard as conscientious scruples against the whole business. It was for this reason that earlier, in Subsubsection 2 (ii) (a), I spoke not simply of a sincere conviction but, more elaborately, of "a principled and disinterested conviction, open to revision or withdrawal in deference to good reasons given".

Generous people often acknowledge the sincerity of the convictions of opponents. Yet that someone when he says that he believes whatever it may be is truthful is by itself no very broad or firm basis for respect. What is much better is that his concern to know the truth, or to do his duty, is so sincere that he is ready to criticise his own ideas, and to take account of objections. If his sincere conviction is presented as a moral conviction, then our respect should wait on the answers to two questions. First, is it principled, in the sense that the same consistent standard is being applied impartially? Second, is it disinterested, in the sense that he would be prepared to make some sacrifice in order to implement it? We all know, or we should all know, what to think of the putative moral objection to the use of napalm or poison gas which evaporates when the weapon is employed by some preferred antagonist. On the other hand we are, or we should be, quick to accept the good conscience of the person who, though he feels he cannot undertake this contentious duty, stands forward to accept some equally or more personally disagreeable alternative.

(b) The point made by Andris in his specification of his watching and correcting Condition 3a is different from the one developed in my Section 2. But they are complementary and partly overlapping rather than in disagreement. My point was that it is an index of sincerity of purpose in teaching that the teacher should be concerned to assess the progress of his pupils. This could be drawn out as a consequence of what Andris specifies as his Condition 3: "Person X is trying by rule-governed behaviour to bring out rule-conforming behaviour in some learner" (p. 236).

His watching and correcting Condition 3a can also, if you again put the emphasis on the trying, be seen as a consequence of his Condition 3; and that he himself numbers it 3a and not 4 suggests, though he does not actually say, that he thinks of it as a derivation from 3. Certainly if you are – sorry, if X is – really trying "to bring about this rule-conforming behaviour", and if "The learner's behaviour is to be corrected by X whenever it is judged by X that such correction may or will result in the desired behaviour", then you are – that is to say, X is – scarcely going to wait until such occasions for salutary correction occur spontaneously.

With appropriate alterations the same applies to intentional learning. For anyone who is trying to learn must take steps to discover whether he is learning it right, and how much progress he is making. He must also be ready to correct himself, or to be corrected, when he has got it wrong. It is often, especially for a beginner, very difficult without assistance to tell whether he is learning it right; and what, if any, progress he is actually making. This is one of the reasons why it is usually useful to have a teacher. But whether intentional learning is to occur with or without intentional teaching there can be no escape in either from some sort of monitoring and assessment of progress, and from the use of the findings of this monitoring and assessment as the occasions and stimuli for further achievement. It is a mark of insincerity of educational purpose to propose either as an educational ideal, or as an educational policy, the abolition of all assessment, and all examinations.

7 Principles and Participation

The present chapter was originally composed in the summer of 1969, while I was still at the University of Keele. Precisely because it was very much an occasional paper I have not in this case made any drastic revisions, excisions or new additions. The only alterations made are of four kinds: first, I have restored some sometimes substantial cuts; second, I have added some notes, mainly to illuminate what the passage of the years may have made obscure; third, I have assimilated the style of the references to persons and sources, and the framework of subheadings and subdivisions, to that followed elsewhere in this book; and fourth, I have inserted one or two cross-references to earlier and later chapters. Some of what remains is in consequence out of date: governments have come and gone and come again, and Edward Short has passed on from the Department of Education to politically higher office; Brian MacArthur too has been promoted to become the first Editor of the *Times Higher Education Supplement*; the Revolutionary Socialist Students' Federation (R.S.S.F.) has dissolved, and the National Union of Students (N.U.S.) has passed from the control of left-wing social democrats into the hands of the 'Broad Left' coalition of Muscovite Communists with their fellow-travellers; and so on. But the main burden of what was said in 1969 and is repeated now is not so ephemeral. For the overriding aim was, and still is, to show that the practical issues in dispute can and should be debated and decided with reference to clearly stated and defensible principles.

1. The Mind of the Minister

It is, unfortunately, topical to start with two views into the mind of Edward Short. The first is provided by an answer to a

Parliamentary question about unruly undergraduates: "Two factors are involved here. The first is the terrible conflicts in society itself. Students would be abnormal if they were not acutely sensitive to these. The second is the fact that many of our universities still do not give students a part in running their own affairs. The concept of a university is that it should be a self-governing body of students, but a great body of the students are not at present able to take part in the governing of their universities" (9 May 1968). A second supplementary insight is mediated by Brian MacArthur, Education Correspondent of *The Times*: "The authoritarian regimes that persisted in too many universities were an important secondary element in student unrest, Mr Short, Secretary of State for Education and Science, told the conference of the Association of Education Committees here today" (29 June 1968). The Minister then, after urging that there should be "new methods of discipline that are more appropriate to the democratic context in which students will live their adult lives", proceeded to tell his Blackpool audience that much of the education provided is "intellectual junk". For it is, it seems he said, "more important to know all the facts about Vietnam than to know the details of the Wars of the Roses. . . . The apparent chaos and violence of student protest, rightly understood and used, could raise the whole quality of our democracy."

Taken together those two utterances are as remarkable as they are, I am afraid, characteristic. They suggest a general philistinism, a particular hostility towards universities, and a reluctance to recognise any of the basic distinctions relevant to a discussion of student participation in the running of institutions of higher education. As regards the general philistinism, it must here suffice to say that it should embarrass all concerned to recognise that the Minister shares his contempt for the supposedly irrelevant past with both that archetypal capitalist entrepreneur Henry Ford the First and the fanatical ultras of the Socialist Society at the London School of Economics (L.S.E.). The former, as everybody knows, dismissed all history as bunk. The latter recently demonstrated at and against a special lecture given by Hugh Trevor-Roper, Regius Professor of Modern History in the University of Oxford, on 'History, Past and Present'. This is, in the words of their pamphlet *Oration or Discussion?*, "a topic which bears no real relation to the issues that face us". (See Max Beloff in *Encounter* for May 1969, p. 69n.)

A particular hostility towards universities is suggested by the Minister's choice of these as his target at Blackpool. For universities in fact are, as indeed they should be, the least authoritarian of all the institutions falling within his sphere. He is not, surely, himself so innocent in politics as to assume that agitation and demonstration vary directly with the extent and seriousness of grievances? In so far as there is any such regular relationship – and I do not believe that there is – it would seem to be not direct but inverse. Thus throughout 1968 – that Year of Academic Revolutions – the noisiest and most persistent uproar among British students came from largely ruleless institutions like Essex and the L.S.E. From all the nearly 160 Colleges of Education, many of which remain notorious for the restrictiveness of their regulations, not one whisper of a sit-in was heard – not one single well-televised shout of 'Che lives!' or 'Student power now!' (See, again, Brian MacArthur in the *Cornmarket Higher Education Review* for Autumn 1968, p. 69.)

Had the Minister at Blackpool chosen to direct his fire at the discipline in these colleges – for which, incidentally, his audience actually had some direct responsibility – he might have got less political mileage, less personal satisfaction, and perhaps less publicity. But he might have done some good.

2.   *The Basic Distinction*

What, however, mainly concerns us here is the reluctance to recognise any of the basic distinctions relevant to a discussion of student participation in the running of institutions of higher education. For some decisions in or for these institutions have been and are being taken with little or no regard to these distinctions. In many places concessions are being devised in order to meet or to anticipate pressures from the Minister or from Parliamentary inquiries, demands from Students' Unions, and even the felt need to be in the fashionable swing with the Sunday supplements. Such concessions are then sold to waverers as really only little ones; as inevitable; as moving with the times; and so on – through the whole litany of the pusillanimous. Yet to act in this way is both shortsighted and, in the most literal sense, unprincipled. The inevitable, as Isaiah Berlin reminds us, is too frequently only what though perfectly avoidable is not in fact resisted (Berlin, pp. 77-8). Moving with, and adjustment to, the times was – it should be remembered more often – the discreditable glory of the Vicar of Bray. The shortsightedness lies in the simple fact that any steps taken without regard to a principle are likely later to be construed as an admission of what was once so conveniently and so comfortably ignored.

(i) The first basic distinctions are those between the qualified and the unqualified, the teachers and the taught. I should blush to spell out fundamentals so obvious if only it were not equally obvious that they are being disregarded. Consider the Short use, in a prepared Parliamentary answer, of the word 'students'. Up to and including the clause in which he asserts "that many of our universities still do not give students a part in running their own affairs" he is referring only to those who are formally under instruction. But then in the premise which is vital to his conclusion, that "The concept of a university is that it should be a self-governing body of students", the word 'student' has, surely, to be taken in a more comprehensive sense. It now covers both those who are elsewhere described as students and the academic staff – in America more happily labelled the faculty. The justification which would presumably be offered for bundling the lot together as all, in a wider sense, students is that the faculty, though qualified and no longer under instruction, still studies as well as teaches. Yet to say that it is, or even that it is part of, the concept of a university as being an institution of teaching and research that it should be, in this artificially widened sense of the word 'student', a self-governing body of students, is much as if you were to say that a teaching hospital should be run by the medicos; and then insisted on interpreting the word 'medicos' to include not only the qualified doctors but also the medical and even the nursing students. (Such collapsings of distinctions between the qualified and the unqualified, or the not yet qualified, provide one more manifestation of that new egalitarianism which I explained and labelled in Subsubsection 1 (ii) (c) of Chapter 6, above.)

(ii) The second set of basic distinctions are those between the academic and the non-academic, between those matters which are the concern of the university as such and those which are by contrast peculiarly the business, whether individually or collectively, of the students. These distinctions are none the less crucial for the fact that there are many mixed and marginal cases in which it is hard or impossible to draw any clear or confident lines. Precisely the same proviso applies to the even more important distinctions between sanity and insanity, riches and poverty, age and youth, or an open society and one in which everything that is not forbidden is compulsory.[20] The fact that a difference is a difference of degree, or that is one with regard to which it is for some other reason not possible always to provide a definite and obviously correct determination, is not a sufficient reason for dismissing the corresponding distinction. Differences of degree are not necessarily, what they are so commonly mistaken to be, mere differences of degree (Flew: 7).

In his own way the Minister himself seems to have been observing as well as confounding the distinctions indicated at the beginning of the previous paragraph. For he starts with the complaint "that many of our universities still do not give students a part in running their own affairs" (where the antecedent of the word 'their' should be students). He is nevertheless going to conclude that the scandal is rather that these same students "are not at present able to take part in the governing of their universities".

(iii) The third set of basic distinctions is between consulting and deciding, between expressing criticisms and making decisions, between making representations to bodies and having representatives on them. The differences are all obvious once they have been noticed. Yet it is easy to miss or to lose these, especially when you employ such equivocal idioms as 'They want a say in this'. Here, however, this Minister cannot be charged with failing to distinguish. For while his predecessor was careful to advocate only the one thing, the present incumbent appears equally unambiguously to support the other. Whereas Anthony Crosland used in this sort of context – though not, I fear, about fees for overseas students[21] – to say "I am anxious for due consultation" (10 February 1967), Edward Short now proclaims that students should "take part in the governing of their universities".

To preserve distinctions of this third group we must, for instance, refuse to accept the mere fact that some representations made were not implemented as sufficient reason for concluding that these representations were not listened to, or were not seriously considered, and were to no effect at all. They may have been listened to most attentively, they may have been given a lot of weight in the consequent deliberations, yet nevertheless – whether rightly or wrongly – overridden by other considerations. Again, although the making of these representations may not have effected the outcome this time, the fact that they were both made and duly noted may still have some effect on future decisions.

Generally we have to recognise – what is today increasingly often overlooked – that the fact that this or that group or cause or interest has not got its way through some procedure is not enough to show that that procedure has failed; and that more militant action is the only and proper alternative. The fact, for instance, that you – or we – have failed to prevent some international sporting or cultural event by orderly and peaceful protest does not by itself show that orderly and peaceful protest has failed; and that the right thing now is to try violently to disrupt the performance which we find so obnoxious. Perhaps the correct moral may be that we have so far failed to get our fellow citizens to share our revulsions, and that we must rededicate ourselves to the long uphill task of peaceful persuasion. At any rate in cases of the sort just now suggested this surely is the moral, since what we presumably want is that an offending foreign government should be confronted by a deep and wide movement of British public opinion – not just with a handful of dedicated, but reckless and unrepresentative militants.

3. *The Place for Participation*

Within universities, although not yet within all those other institutions of tertiary education of which the Minister was carefully not talking, there is no disagreement in principle with the proposition that there should be elected student representatives serving as full members of a great many of the decision-making bodies. Thus the National Union of Students and the Committee of Vice-Chancellors and Principals had no difficulty in their recent *Joint Statement* in agreeing: that in "the whole field of student welfare – for example health services, catering facilities and the provision of accommodation – ... there should ... be varying degrees of participation of students in the decision-making process"; and that there is also the area of "the operation of student unions and the management of a wide range of extracurricular activities, in which most university student organizations rightly have long had complete responsibility".

Within this relatively undisputatious field there are still general points worth making. First, it is indeed overtime that the practices which have been long established in the universities were extended to all the other tertiary institutions. Second, one is constantly confronted by difficulties arising from the fundamental fact that student generations are short. Student members of any committee have to serve for terms which may be too abbreviated for efficiency. Student representatives are likely to be involved in making decisions which will affect only the constituents of their successors. Third, the forthcoming reduction of the age of majority to eighteen will ensure that the buck will stop where it belongs. For all undergraduates will become competent to make enforceable contracts in their own right. Fourth, this development and some others facilitate a policy of hiving off some peripheral university commitments to autonomous bodies wholly under student control.

For instance, several universities, unable any longer to obtain public money to pay for building more halls of residence, are already exploring with their Students' Unions the possibilities of financing these by private loans to student housing associations. If this welcome initiative proves successful we could surely also then sell off to other similarly financed student co-operatives some at least of those existing halls of residence which are on sites isolated from the main campus. Such devolutions from centralised control might be the universities' analogue of the policy, which I hope the next Conservative government will press strenuously, of offloading the nationalised oddments – the brickworks of the National Coal Board, the 51 per cent state interest in British Petroleum, the public houses of Carlisle, and so on.

Next, and without prejudice to any questions of proper membership and appointment, it should be undisputed common ground that all those who have to make decisions, whether as individuals or as members of bodies, ought to hear attentively and genuinely to consider representations from those affected by their decisions. To do this is part of what is involved in respecting people as human beings; and a recognition of this sort of equality entails no requirement to disregard, or to deny, or to strive to abolish, all inequalities of fortune, or of talents, or of qualifications. (See, again, Subsubsection 1 (ii) (c) of Chapter 6, above.)

To establish machinery for making representations, and then making this machinery work, is in any large and complex organisation a big and awkward job. It is also – like painting the Forth railway bridge – one which is never finished. It will often be the case, and much more often be believed to be, that the machinery is inadequate or that it is not being sincerely worked. For considering representations is time-consuming, and can be upsetting; while those whose case has been considered and rejected are always humanly inclined to believe that had it truly been considered it could not have been rejected.

These are all no doubt truisms. Their reiteration may be partly excused by quoting the First Maxim for Balliol Men: 'Even a truism may be true'. They are also specially relevant to our universities, which have in recent years grown enormously. In, for instance, a small department casual social contacts, buttonholing, and dropping in may ensure that information is spread and representations are heard. Once a department is grown so large that the office of its Head has to be guarded by a secretarial Cerberus, then perhaps the time has come to create a Staff–Student Consultative Committee. When this has become necessary in some departments it is not by that token either essential or desirable to make the same machinery a mandatory imposition upon all, however small: the notion that what any need all must have is as misguided as – though less mean, less envious, and so less popular than – the proposition that no one ought to have anything which not everyone has or can have. This need in a large department for such formal machinery must be accounted one of the extravagances of scale. When comparing the efficiencies of large as opposed to small organisations these extravagances should be, yet too rarely are, put in the balance against the economies; and not in higher education only.

4. *The Area of Dispute*

About two important matters there is, as we have seen, no disagreement in theory. Certainly university – and not, I'd say, only university – students should have the lion's share "in running their own affairs". Certainly too there must everywhere be channels through which they, like everybody else, can make their representations heard. Of course, in practice there is still plenty to be done under both heads despite the theoretical consensus. But the issues of contested principle lie elsewhere, in the second area distinguished by the *Joint Statement* – "that relating . . . to curriculum and courses, teaching methods, major organizational matters, and issues concerning the planning and development of the university".

Here the N.U.S. and the Vice-Chancellors agreed to be non-committal: "the ultimate decision must be that of the statutorily responsible body"; although it is "essential that students' views should be properly taken into account". The contested issue of principle arises at precisely the point where this statement stops. The questions are whether there should be student representative members – and, if so, whether these should number a substantial proportion – of these bodies. The issues are complicated slightly by the fact that it is still generally, though not quite universally, allowed that there is a third area to which students should on no account be admitted; that of "decisions on appointments, promotions, and . . . the personal position of members of staff, the admission of individuals and their academic assessment". The conflict has been intensified by the latest conference of the N.U.S., which replaced the officers who had signed the *Joint Statement* by more militant successors, and endorsed claims for substantial – say one-third – student membership of Councils and Senates.

About Councils, which leave all purely academic matters to their Senates, I will say only that the shortness of the student stay in the university should surely be by itself sufficient to rule out of further consideration any but a token representation.

It is on the Senate and its academic committees that the crucial issues of academic self-government hinge. For it is these which are ultimately responsible for teaching and research, the essential and defining activities of a university as such. And the claim of Senate to autonomy within its province – a claim jealously defended when necessary both against lay members of Council and against incursions from the outside world – rests upon the fact that it is a special sort of professional body, consisting of people duly qualified and occupationally committed to the business of the university.

Anyone, therefore, who is going to suggest that such bodies should be diluted by the admission of student members needs to field strong argument. For these members will be people who have not qualified, who are still under instruction ultimately supervised by these very bodies, and whose involvement in the university must be presumed to be strictly temporary. Yet the arguments which supporters have been willing to write down are, as far as I have been able to discover, noticeably feeble.

The most seductive is, perhaps, a general democratic appeal – that all government should be controlled by the governed, either directly or through representatives. When this is put by members of the R.S.S.F. it is tempting to counter with some appropriately hostile reference to the practice, and even the theory, of the now very numerous socialist countries. (Solid supporters of our Labour Party might also, not altogether ineptly, be reminded of their present Gerrymander Bill.)[22] But it is more constructive, if less satisfying, to challenge the implicit analogy between a university and a country or a local government area. Surely being a teaching institution must make a crucial difference, at least as regards all matters involving the teacher–taught relation? And surely, again, there is a far closer analogy with a specialist club or professional body which may, without offence to any democratic principles, require certain qualifications for full voting membership?[23]

Protagonists of *Student Power* are fond of at least some industrial analogies, and they like to think that their kind of students are the natural allies of the industrial working class (Cockburn and Blackburn, passim). It may do scant justice to the profundities of this piece of social analysis to point out that during the troubles at Keele in 1968 members of the cleaning and catering staff, many of them wives of Silverdale miners, were far more vehement in their advocacy of a strong disciplinary response than any of the 'academic bosses'. But certainly it should be seen as paradoxical that the noisiest demands for 'participation' and for 'workers' control' have been coming from some of those who have not yet completed their training. For if there are any positive analogies between a university and a factory, then the true analogue of the university student is not the skilled craftsman in his trades union but the apprentice. Or, since one of the products of a university is graduates, a still more appropriate analogue is whatever it is which the factory is engaged in shaping into something else.

Having said this I must expect (descriptive) to be misreported as having said that a university is or ought to be merely a factory, and that the students are merely its raw materials. Of course this would be a misrepresentation. To say that this is in certain respects like that is not to say that this is that. Rather it is to take it for granted that this is not that, that besides the similarities mentioned there are also dissimilarities. In the case of the analogy between the student and "whatever it is which the factory is engaged in shaping into something else", the first and most enormously important difference is that the student is a person.

Another fallacy common here is to argue that all the constituent institutions of a democratic society must themselves be democratic, that in the army of a truly democratic state there would either be no officers or only elected officers, and so on. There is no doubt but that this argument, so confidently trumpeted from a hundred platforms, is fallacious. It is fallacious because it does not follow that whatever is characteristic of a complex must be characteristic of its components also: a heap may be large and heavy though it is a heap of fine sand. This fallacy even has a traditional name, the Sorites (pronounced, So-wry-tees) or Heap.

But though it is unsound, as a matter of logic, to argue that all the constituent institutions of a democratic society must themselves be democratic, it is realistic to recognise, as a matter of fact, that the democracy of a democratic state will be precarious unless that state contains a great many other democratic institutions. The National Socialists in Germany knew what they were about when, with opposite intentions, they insisted that not only must the will of the leader Adolf Hitler be supreme in the state but the same Leader-principle must be applied in the running of local government and of private clubs. Since, however, the Sorites is a fallacy, and since we cannot simply deduce from a commitment to democracy at the national level commitments to the running of every single subordinate institution in the same way, it remains, even for those of us most committed to the democratic state, a further question which other institutions ought to be run democratically, and what is the appropriate electorate in each particular case. It certainly cannot be taken as an immediate and obvious consequence of fundamental democratic principle that, for instance, the army of a democratic state should be subject to democratic controls exercised by the soldiers as such, or even that in those other institutions which certainly should be democratically run the appropriate electorate consists of all those who are in any way involved as members or associate members, owners, customers, employees, or what have you.

The suggestion continually made is that democratic principles require that students be represented on the Senates and all other governing bodies of the institutions of which they are studying. Coming from the Leninist R.S.S.F. and its like, appeals to democratic principle are a little hard to take. But as I have tried to show, the reasons usually offered in support of this suggestion are in any case not sufficient. If they were, then it would be impossible to deny the claim of Action for a Free University – the ebullient but short-lived Keele student power pressure group – that the students, the faculty, and all others entitled to representation, must be entitled to it on a strictly one man one vote and no weighting basis. To admit any students as representatives is bound sooner or later to be construed as the thin end of this gigantic wedge; and not unreasonably. No wonder that Trevor Fisk as President of the N.U.S. seized on another later statement by Edward Short: that "there is a danger that students are becoming second-class citizens in their college community". (*Universities Quarterly*, 1967-8, p. 392.)

Certainly if any such analogy with national citizenship is allowed, then any student representation not in proportion to the relative numbers of students and faculty becomes a Rhodesian constitutional scandal. But this analogy is question-begging, and cannot be allowed to pass unchallenged. Equality of citizen rights for all adult citizens does not entail, as this analogy assumes, that every adult citizen must at every stage in life enjoy exactly the same rights and status with respect to every institution as every other adult citizen. It is not enough to appeal to the principle of equal national citizenship in order to derive the conclusion that there must be no probationary or associate or other multi-tier membership of anything. Demagogic talk about second-class citizenship should – and, I feel pretty sure, would – cut no ice in a discussion of whether the apprentices are to be immediately admitted as full members of the craft union which they are at present training to become qualified to join. There is no inconsistency, and no scandal to democratic principle, in the fact that Oxford and Cambridge have both senior and junior members, with very different and unequal rights and duties within and towards their university; notwithstanding that, as adult citizens of the United Kingdom, their legal rights and duties are the same.

5.   *Some Committee Reports*

Imre Lakatos, writing of the two reports of a faculty–student Machinery of Government Committee at L.S.E., asserts: "There is not a single argument in the Majority Report as to *why* students should be admitted to Senate and Council; nor are obvious counter-arguments refuted or even mentioned" (Cox and Dyson: 1, p. 29; authors' italics). The University of Keele recently received similar Majority and Minority reports from a similar committee. Here too the former was far less fundamental than the latter; and here too the Majority were significantly careful not even to state, much less to try to explain why they had themselves come now to reject, the traditional appeals to the academic qualifications and the long-term professional commitment of the faculty. But they did in their fashion outdo their opposite numbers at the L.S.E. by offering two general reasons in support of their proposals, which included recommendations to introduce student representatives into Senate and its key academic committees. (They were to have had between a fifth and a sixth of the resulting membership.)

(i) The first reason was: "The committee adopted as its ideal the establishment of a working partnership between all people forming the University community at Keele." Nothing whatsoever was said to explain why this ideal demanded representation for students but not, apparently, for any of the non-academic employees of the University. Nor – notwithstanding that our Professor of Law was a most enthusiastic member of the Majority Reporters – was there any thought of asking after the professional qualifications of the proposed new partners. We thus have one more example of using a term in a weak sense in the first step of an argument, and not noticing that you need something much stronger to warrant the desired conclusion. Of course we want everyone who works here, technicians and domestics just as much as students, to feel in some way part of the place. But from this it does not follow that they have the qualifications needed to become partners in running its academic business.

It is perhaps significant that, in the sentence immediately following, the Majority Report asserts that: "Its conclusions and recommendations should be read as contributions towards that aim rather than as 'concessions' invented to meet 'demands'." Certainly the militants of the Minority Report were not alone in believing that this was the studiously denied, but to some decisive, third consideration.[24] They could, and did, point to the facts: that the Exploratory Committee was originally set up in a threatening rumble of demonstrations to come; that soon afterwards our first sit-in, led by officers of the Students' Union, 'took over the Registry'; and that the same Union after the crucial proposals had been rejected issued a menacing and memorably unbalanced manifesto. In this the Senate verdict was described as, among other things: "an insult to this Union . . . a dangerous decision . . . ignoring the case made by the Committee . . . taking a totally authoritarian line . . . such high-handed action by this authoritarian body constitutes an abominable and total repudiation of any pretence this university has to being a liberal institution."

(ii) The second argument in that supposed case read: "student membership . . . was both desirable and useful because of the experience and interests represented which could contribute towards the discussion of items of business and their successful resolution." This too lacks both punch and particularity. The question to be pressed – as so often when experience is mentioned – is: 'What experience?'; or – hastily – 'What relevant experience?'

Curiously this Majority Report hinted a damping answer. For its student members – unprotestingly accompanied by their faculty fellow-travellers – insisted on starting by talking about assessment, although this scarcely fell within their terms of reference. It would be hard to find a better instance of academic business on which any student's experience must be wretchedly narrow compared with that of his teachers. For the student has yet to take his finals, and has never examined. But any Senate as already constituted can, at the drop of a hat, set up its working party on examinations manned by qualified people all of whom have themselves at some stage been through the whole examination mill, and all of whom have examined recently in other places and under other systems.[25]

This second argument of the Keele Majority Report does nevertheless at least suggest what is the best reason I know for having a student on Senate. It might be labelled the Memento Mori Argument. A large part of the function of the academic profession is to get students to learn, just as the whole point of the medical profession is to help patients to become and stay well. Yet members of both may, being human, from time become in some way forgetful or neglectful of this truth. It was perhaps with this in mind that some universities – long ago, before any of today's young agitators or old conservatives were born – arranged to have on their Senates the President of their Students' Union.

Unfortunately in the present context of conflict it would, I think, be impossible for others to do the same; and then halt. Drawing lines between the qualified and the teacher on the one side and the unqualified student on the other, and then between the academic and the non-academic, you have a rationale which is easy to defend because it is easily seen and understood. And yet there is a world of difference between the single officer sitting as such and the panel of elected representatives or – all too likely – delegates.

There may be a place for one skull in the hermit's cell. But a whole charnel-house is quite another thing.

8 Academic Freedoms and Academic Purposes

The main purpose of this final chapter is to develop and defend the thesis that if there is to be anything special about academic freedom, as opposed to freedom without prefix or suffix, or if there is to be any separate and distinctive justification for this special sort of freedom, then the peculiarities will have to be grounded in the distinctiveness of academic duties and academic functions. But since the most recent and most widely circulated British book on *Academic Freedom* is to my mind full of damaging error, and since the professed concern of its sponsors seems always to be subordinate to a primary and often incompatible political commitment to a Radical collectivism, the chapter takes the form of a polemic against that book.

Anthony Arblaster, now a Lecturer in Politics in the University of Sheffield, tells us that he wrote *Academic Freedom* "at the request of the Executive Committee of the Council for Academic Freedom and Democracy (CAFD)", of which he is a founder member. The preface continues: 'In view of its subject matter, it is ironic that this book should be one of the very last to be produced by Penguin Education, the division which was abruptly closed down by Pearson Longman in February 1974." There follows a dark warning against "an organization controlled by a financial group of this kind", the first of many hostile references to the demon capitalism.

Certainly a word does need to be said about the fact that a work such as this "should be one of the very last produced by Penguin Education"; and that it was written with help from "my Penguin editor, Jonathan Croall", who did so much to make that division what it was. But, rather than Arblaster's word 'ironic', an apter phrase would be 'entirely true to form'. Something needs to be said too about C.A.F.D. For that organisation gets considerable publicity in the educational press and elsewhere. It is often treated as if it were an outfit straightforwardly dedicated to the objects stated in its title. Most remarkably, the *Times Higher Education Supplement* permits it to supply its own monthly 'C.A.F.D. Column'. Nevertheless, as I shall give reason for saying, C.A.F.D. corporately and several of its most prominent members individually earn the reproach of A. Phillips Griffiths, Professor of Philosophy in the University of Warwick. He wrote: "I find that many of the specific conclusions I draw are very different from those reached by persons usually most vocal in defence of what they take to be academic freedom. I would regard most of them as the enemies of it."[26]

1.   *Two Concepts of Academic Freedom*

On one fundamental Arblaster and I are in agreement. He does accept that any notion of academic freedom must be rooted in the nature of the peculiarly academic functions, and hence that a theoretical treatment has to start from some understanding of these. His trouble – and ours – is that he does not see their nature clearly enough. Nor, it appears, does he care very much about them. Like so many of the Penguin Educators his own predominant interests are quite obviously much more in exploiting educational institutions to produce Radical social change (which, being interpreted, is socialism).

(i) His first chapter is entitled, impeccably, 'Academic Freedom: The Educational Case'. But before we actually reach this we have paragraphs expressing Arblaster's monocular and curiously paranoiac vision of contemporary Britain: "Academic freedom . . . is today under threat from several quarters, and urgently needs to be defended. . . . Sooner or later a choice will have to be made between greater freedom and democracy, or less. There are signs that our rulers have already made their choice – for repression. . . . Dissent, whether peaceable or not, becomes increasingly suspect and risky. The attempts, often successful, to exclude or expel radical students and staff from the educational system form one element in this overall pattern" (p. 9).

The case itself begins with the statement: "Freedom is a concept that ought to provoke questions, not merely routine assent; and the crucial questions are always – freedom for whom, in practice? and from what, to do what?" (p. 11).

Furthermore, he continues, "freedom is always freedom *to do* something" (p. 13: italics his). So what, on Arblaster's view, is academic freedom the freedom *to do*? "The freedom that matters", he explains, "is the openness of education, that is, the tolerance of a great range and diversity of approaches and opinions, not only in relation to specific subjects, but also in relation to education itself, its purposes and methods. This implies that students and children ought to be free to pursue what is important or interesting to them, and that teachers should be free to use the methods and put forward the interpretations which they believe in. In education the freedom to hold opinions, especially unorthodox opinions, and to advocate them openly and without any fear of reprisal, is supremely important" (pp. 13-14). Again: "The freedom that matters is the freedom to teach and to learn according to one's convictions and interests" (p. 15).

With much of this, as far as it goes, I wholeheartedly concur. And, with that same crucial caveat, much of it would be equally acceptable to those whom Arblaster peremptorily dismisses as "reactionary professors like Max Beloff, Donald MacRae and Peter Wiles" (p. 162)[27]. Here I would say two things only. First: it must not be taken as given – much less as obvious – that at every age children should enjoy the same freedom of choice between alternative subjects of study, and between alternative areas of concentration within subjects, as is or should be granted to adult university students. Second: I hope, yet scarcely expect, that Arblaster accepts that his own stated principles of academic freedom forbid the compulsory imposition of a uniform national system of unstreamed comprehensive schools: or, for that matter, any other uniform national system. (This we may in charity still hope, since Arblaster's contribution to that earlier Penguin manifesto, *Education for Democracy*, was confined to 'Education and Ideology': Rubinstein and Stoneman, pp. 34-40[28].)

But what is so important in Arblaster's account of academic functions and academic freedoms, and what is so revealing, is what it leaves out. It shows no concern for knowledge. There is no mention of the need to shape and to reshape opinions and convictions in the light of the evidence. There is no insistence upon the consequent duty of critical, and above all of self-critical, rationality. The maximum concession to the demands of academic discipline permitted by Arblaster's other and prior commitments is memorably grudging. It comes in a paragraph urging that "neutrality, or impartiality . . . is an absurdity". He says: "Objectivity, in the sense of a respect for facts, and a certain standard of honesty in the treatment of evidence, is an obviously desirable quality for education to cultivate" (p. 17).

(ii) Next, in salutary contrast, consider some things said by the Polish philosopher Ajdukiewicz. Along with all his compatriots he has had far more direct experience of constraints on academic freedom than any homekeeping Englishman: first under the Polish colonels; then under the Germans; and finally, since the Russian occupation, in what I once heard a historian in Warsaw describe, without a flicker of embarrassment, as "the period of People's Poland". Ajdukiewicz begins in the present context by distinguishing four freedoms: freedom of choice of subject of inquiry; freedom of method of inquiry; freedom of thought; and freedom of speech.

He at once links these academic rights with academic functions and academic duties. This distinctively "scientific freedom does not mean a freedom of speech so unrestricted that it would permit the dissemination of rubbish or unintelligible gibberish". So, correspondingly, freedom of thought implies "a right to believe in that and only that which can be rationally justified, and a right to disbelieve everything that is not supported by rational argument and, even more so, everything that rational argument actually speaks against". So for Ajdukiewicz questions about academic freedom of speech, as opposed to freedom of speech in general, arise only when and in so far as we have meaningful, coherent and rational discourse: an expression of "the competence of the author in the given field" (Skolimowski, p. 135). Ajdukiewicz, therefore, would have agreed with six good words from Chairman Mao: "No investigation, no right to speak" (Mao Tse-tung, p. 230).

Of course this statement by Ajdukiewicz is only a beginning, although it does possess the great merit of being a beginning in the right direction. In particular, it needs to be in some way extended or spelt out to cover duties to students, and the duties and rights of students. Clearly the "right to believe in that and only that which can be rationally justified" must apply equally to the student, likewise the duty to seek and to cherish truth.

Clearly too the teacher's duties to competence and to the subject are duties to his students also. It is neither his right nor his duty to present to those in his care any opinions – whether orthodox or unorthodox – except in a dedicated and disciplined concern for whatever is best evidenced and nearest to the truth. Nor can it be among his duties to them an optional, albeit obviously desirable, extra to strive for "Objectivity, in the sense of a respect for facts, and . . . honesty in the treatment of evidence". These things are all imperatively required, not only by commitment to the basic objects of the whole academic exercise, but also by respect of our students, who are not to be deceived or in any other way intellectually short-changed.

Maybe Ajdukiewicz should have said a little more. But there is another all too likely objection which would be entirely mistaken. Nothing which Ajdukiewicz says about limitations on academic freedoms, and nothing which his statements may suggest about the proper justification for such distinctively academic freedoms, should be construed as implying that anything – much less everything – which fails to satisfy his stringent specifications for academic discourse ought to be suppressed.

The crux to seize is, as I said earlier, "that if there is to be anything special about academic freedom . . ., or if there is to be any separate and distinctive justification for this special sort of freedom, then the peculiarities will have to be grounded in the distinctiveness of academic duties and academic functions". But to insist on this is neither to say nor to suggest: either that no one, whether academic or non-academic, ought to enjoy any freedoms other than academic freedoms; or that there is no justification for any freedoms for anyone, whether non-academic or academic, which is not grounded in the nature of the peculiar academic functions.

(iii) The value and relevance to us of these statements by Ajdukiewicz lie in two things. In the first place they propose a firm linking of academic rights with academic duties. Such linkings are always desirable: we should all of us always before demanding, fashionably, our rights ask ourselves, unfashionably, how far we are fulfilling our duties. Sometimes too the possession of a moral right, if not a legal right, is itself contingent upon the fulfilment of some corresponding duty: my moral, though not my legal, right to publish my findings ought to be seen as conditional upon my having done a thorough and conscientious job of investigation and exposition. Again, moral rights to various civil liberties, though not by the same token legal rights, ought to be seen as contingent upon a willingness to reciprocate.

(a) This last is a highly topical point of principle. The Vice-Chancellor of Lancaster recently protested: "Those champions of the liberties of the left who last year, in my presence, attempted to howl down a speaker from the Monday Club, stand convicted of not knowing what freedom is about, or of hypocrisy in their championship of it." (*T.H.E.S.*, 17 November 1972). A Lecturer from the same university, himself a longtime self-confessed member of the Communist Party (Muscovite), was elsewhere in the same issue reported as complaining at the Annual General Meeting of C.A.F.D. that "Lancaster University had become a nicely landscaped concentration camp". I do not know whether he was also active in the flesh on the occasion referred to by his Vice-Chancellor, or only in spirit. In that case the University authorities for once made so bold as temporarily to forbid two of the offenders to attend further political meetings on campus. Had the principle thus exemplified been appreciated more widely there would have been less foolish embarrassment and misdirected indignation at this most fitting punishment. As it was the local branch of the N.U.S. went overboard in demanding an end to such intolerable "victimization". A disciple once asked that currently disfavoured sage Confucius whether his rule of conduct might not be epitomised in a single word: "The master replied, 'Is not "reciprocity" the word?' " (*Analects,* xv § 23).

Curiously it was only two years later that the N.U.S. nationally at their 1974 conference apparently accepted the principle which their Lancaster local branch had earlier so clearly rejected. For that conference carried overwhelmingly a resolution to prevent "by whatever means are necessary" in any institutions of tertiary education any meetings to be addressed by any speakers whom the N.U.S. local affiliate should deem to be "racialist or fascist"; and the main argument in the main and deliriously applauded supporting speech was that there is no democratic obligation, nor is it at this time prudent, to permit the freedoms of free society to be exploited by those labouring to overthrow such a society and to abolish all such freedoms for their opponents. The speaker, Steve Parry, the then Secretary, made much of the effective abuse by the National Socialists of the liberties of the Weimar Republic.

Yet this first appearance of approval for Confucian moral principle was deceptive. For the embargo was specifically intended to apply only to alleged "racialists and fascists"; most of whom, incidentally, are in fact neither racialist nor fascist[29]. It was also obscenely clear that it was not intended to apply to any of the various sorts of Marxist–Leninist who thronged the conference hall. Some sign of the critical level of the proceedings is provided by the fact that no one present seemed to notice anything incongruous about their Secretary's appeal to this excellent Confucian principle; notwithstanding that everyone knew that he too is a member of the Communist Party (Muscovite)[30].

(b) Back now to Ajdukiewicz. For us his second contribution is to suggest that the duties which arise from a commitment to the primary academic function – the pursuit of knowledge – are to investigate, to take account of all the evidence, to be systematically rational, to have a competence in some chosen field. All such emphases are conspicuously wanting in Arblaster's account. Although he does concede that "Objectivity . . . is an obviously desirable quality for education to cultivate", there is – and this too I said before – "no concern about actually getting it right . . . no mention of the need to shape and to reshape opinions . . . in the light of the evidence . . . no insistence upon the consequent duty of critical, and above all self-critical, rationality".

As for the idea of competence in some chosen field, it is anathema. Arblaster quotes with horrified distaste from "Sir Michael Swann . . . now ominously elevated to the full-time Chairmanship of the BBC's Board of Governors" (p. 15). Swann wrote in *Black Paper Two*, in Arblaster's eyes monstrously, that " 'the plain fact of the matter is that, inadequate as we may be in other respects, where our own subjects are concerned we *do* know more, and we *do* know better than our students. And I believe we should have the courage to say so' " (p. 147: italics original). Arblaster comments, falsely: "Such a confidently superior approach leaves little room for debate about the proper methods of learning either" (p. 16).

The vital lesson for us to grasp is that the emphases on

evidence, on rationality, on criticism, and even the reference to
areas of competence, all derive directly from the fundamental
academic concern to know, to learn, and to teach the truth. The
fundamental philosophical points are as simple as they are
important. To know it is necessary but not sufficient to be right:
the lucky punter who simply picked Lover Boy as the winner of
the two-thirty with a pin, and turned out to have picked right,
did not know that Lover Boy would win. To know one has also to
be in a position to know: and that, with exceptions which we may
here ignore as irrelevant, means having evidence and reasons.

Criticism, and above all self-criticism, is essential to the pursuit
of knowledge; because we are none of us infallible. It is as easy as
it is common for some ill-founded or even demonstrably
erroneous opinion to pass as knowledge. Our only but never
sure safeguard is strenuous, unresting, rational, and always
truth-directed criticism. To be in this full sense critical it is
neither necessary nor sufficient to repudiate what is thus
criticised. Criticism must sometimes end in at least temporary
acceptance, while simply to reject is not to criticise at all.

(iv) Immanuel Kant once remarked that he had "found it
necessary to deny *knowledge* in order to make room for *faith*"
(Kant: 1, p. 29; italics original). We could with almost equal truth
say of Arblaster that he finds it necessary to deny *knowledge* in
order to make room for *student power*. As he put it in his article
'Education and Ideology', mentioned at the beginning of the
present Section 1, "it is the word 'democracy' which identifies
the Council's . . . Radical position" (Rubinstein and Stoneman,
p. 40).

Writing in *Academic Freedom*, about deciding "what shall be
taught and how", Arblaster affirms: "Students have as much
right to a determining role in these matters as staff." He
continues: "If education is seen primarily as the transmission of
a body of fixed and certain knowledge by informed teachers to
uninformed students, then the idea that students should be free
to determine what shall be taught will be seen as inappropriate
and academically damaging" (p. 15). Indeed it will; especially if
we take care to remove the heavy hostile bias from Arblaster's
presentations of the conservative position. So, given Arblaster's
preposterous commitment to student power, there is nothing
for it but a correspondingly preposterous de-emphasis on the

place in education of any and every form of knowledge, and of the disciplines demanded by the pursuit of knowledge.

So this is what we have. After the momentary relief of reading those scandalous words from Swann we go on to hear: that "education is less concerned with the transmission of a set body of facts – and of course this varies from subject to subject – than with the development of the thought, feelings, and ability of the student" (p. 16); "that education is not, beyond a certain basic level, about the transmission of information so much as getting people to think and find out for themselves, and so teach themselves" (p. 16); and that "The role of theory, or hypothesis, and interpretation is now generally accepted to be an irreducible element in even the most dispassionate and factual sciences" (p. 17); and so on.

But these antitheses do not, as writers on education so often suggest, refer to separable alternatives. We cannot think of developing the capacity and the inclination to find out for oneself without reference to possible objects of knowledge: such as propositions, which are, and can be known to be, true or false; or arguments, which are, and can be known to be, valid or invalid. This capacity and this inclination themselves can be, and usually have to be, taught and inspired by those who are already more proficient; while that proficiency is in its turn another form of knowledge. Theories or hypotheses too, and interpretations, are worthless save in so far as they refer to and serve to explain or otherwise illuminate what is actually the case. And even if they cannot in principle be shown to be true, they certainly can be shown, and known, to be false, or otherwise wrong. So here too there is room for knowledge, as opposed to mere opinion or conviction (Popper: 2 and 3).

Arblaster returns to the charge later, as part of a reply to "politicians, pundits, professors, and principals" (p. 154). He quotes "two openly élitist Lecturers from Hull University". They dared to write: "A university is not, and was never intended to be, a democratic institution. By the very nature of what they are attempting to achieve universities . . . cannot be ruled by the ignorant. . . .". To this Arblaster responds: "Such claims . . . depend upon [a] specious analogy with the possession of expertise in more technical fields." But here is no analogy, specious or otherwise. The claim, and the truth, just is that qualified staff as such have expertise in precisely those fields in which Arblaster is maintaining that "students have as much as staff to contribute to the making of appointments and the designing of courses" (p. 155). If in Arblaster's own present field, or any other, there really is no expertise; then what are he and his present colleagues or those others being paid for?

Furthermore, if people are to be denounced and dismissed as élitists then we – and they – are entitled to some explanation of what an élitist is, and why élitism is supposed to be a bad thing. To state, as I did in Subsection 3 (ii) of Chapter 2, that the Plato of *The Republic* was an arch-élitist makes fairly self-evident sense. For, one hopes, everyone in Edbiz knows that Plato there advocates absolute power for a highly trained physical and intellectual élite, of which all, but only, those – of either sex – who have the necessary genetic endowment can qualify as members. But that cannot be the point here: the terrible two from Hull are not advocating the replacement of our parliamentary democracy by the rule of a new class of Guardians; and Arblaster's Leninist associates in C.A.F.D. certainly do not share my own objection to the absolute, irremovable, uncriticisable rule of a power élite. On the contrary: the establishment of such a system is what Leninism is about. (I apologise for harping on this theme, but so much of the composition and activity of C.A.F.D. does make this harping unavoidably relevant. See, in addition to the other references given earlier or later, materials, including editorials, in the *T.H.E.S.* for 1 and 15 June 1973, 23 November 1973 and 3 May 1974.)

But if, on the other hand, the supposed fault of these two unnamed Hull Lecturers is to believe that special rights and responsibilities should sometimes attach to special skills and qualifications, then we are left at a loss to conjecture any reason why this should be thought always and as such evil. It is, presumably, one more expression of the revolutionary new egalitarianism.

2.   *Further Observations on Penguin Academic Freedom*

The main object of the present chapter was to underline certain consequences of the rather obvious point that any special concept of or case for academic freedom has to be grounded in the distinctiveness of academic duties and academic functions.

But there are some other worthwhile points which arise from Arblaster's book.

(i) One characteristic, albeit peripheral, example of Arblaster's slovenliness is his equation of equality of opportunity with what he commends as the Robbins principle that everyone achieving some minimum level of qualification should be provided with the university course of their choice. Arblaster therefore denounces any failure or refusal to provide places to satisfy all such student demand as a defection from perfect equality of opportunity. He does this without so much as mentioning the here essential question – whether whatever places are available are or are not open to public competition. He thus has his cue for an orgy of sneering indignation against the betrayal of an ideal "which has been one of the central commonplaces of bourgeois society since the time of Cromwell's New Model Army" (p. 148).

Another, perhaps more illuminating, way of looking at this confusion is in terms of a distinction between equality of opportunity at any point in time, and equality of opportunity through time. What is traditionally and ordinarily called equality of opportunity is the former; and it is a matter of whatever positions from time to time become available being open then to all comers in fair competition. The latter is a matter of the chances of getting a position of such and such a kind being the same at different times: if more, or fewer, were born in the year of your birth; then there must be proportionately more, or fewer, of every kind of university place, and of every other sort of position. No wonder that, to Arblaster's distress, "The UGC [University Grants Committee] has made no secret of its dislike of the idea" (p. 148).

(ii) Another, more immediately relevant, example of the collapsing of a crucial distinction comes in the treatment of the contention that "The crime of Atkinson, Blackburn, Bateson, Arblaster, and the teachers at Hornsey and Guildford consisted not in the views they held, but in trying to advance these views through disruption and unconstitutional activities" (p. 117). The standard C.A.F.D. line is that all these people have in fact been persecuted, and for their opinions only; C.A.F.D. spokesmen are especially fond of suggesting that anyone who refuses to join their protests against any of these alleged persecutions is a hypocrite about academic freedom. What is apparently never envisaged, or at any rate never admitted, is that there is well-informed dissent from orthodox C.A.F.D. doctrine on some if not all these various affairs. (See, for instance, the exchanges between Griffith and Westergaard for C.A.F.D. and Peter Child, and again between Arblaster and Peter Child, in the correspondence columns of the *T.H.E.S.*, 18 and 25 May 1973, and 8 and 15 June 1973.) Arblaster, however, insists on construing the refusal of the Association of University Teachers (A.U.T.) to accept all these C.A.F.D. stories as evidence of 'The Teachers' Failure'. So, "the part played by teachers in tertiary education in defending academic freedom has been secondary to that played by the mass of students" (p. 141).

But Arblaster also wants to challenge the distinction upon which the present contention is based: "it must be said that the implication that there can be freedom of speech but not necessarily freedom of action clearly reduces freedom of speech to an ineffectual charade" (p. 118).

In a cool hour, even he would surely see that to permit freedom of opinion while drawing the line at "disruption and unconstitutional activities" does not carry the implication that no one may act on his opinions in any way at all. It is "in the present time", lamentably, sometimes a duty, and not – as Arblaster assumes – a scandalous violation of academic freedom for "a senior lecturer in Sociology" to ask a referee to " 'confirm that Mr. X is not . . . wishing to do sociological research merely to give him an opportunity to disrupt universities' " (p. 103).

(iii) Arblaster was of course writing before the N.U.S. nationally adopted the policy described in Subsubsection 1 (iii)(a), above. Yet there had already been many sporadic incidents of the kind described by the Vice-Chancellor of Lancaster. Arblaster nevertheless pooh-poohs – with his usual references to "professional student-haters" and "reactionary professors and *Black Paper* contributors adding their individual cadenzas of hostility to this chorus of abuse" (pp. 167 and 29) – suggestions that some students may sometimes "represent a threat to freedom of speech in higher education" (p. 164). He concludes: "Behind all the agitated babbling about 'mob rule' lies the fear and hostility of those who see in student demands for educational democracy a threat not to freedom but to their own established power and privileges" (p. 171).

Arblaster actually welcomes the hounding and howling down

of "right-wing Conservative MPs". For "In several of these incidents the 'victim' has been one of a small group . . . including Patrick Wall, Ronald Bell and John Biggs-Davidson". And "if the public learns from the students to treat the politicians with less deference than they have up till now, that will be a gain to democracy and not a loss" (pp. 164 and 165: the sneer quotes for the victims are, predictably, Arblaster's). I wish I could report, in charity towards the author if not in the interests of democracy, that he had proceeded to exclaim: 'Roll on the day when the same treatment is dished out to the massed ranks of the Tribune Group." Clearly, however, the answer to "the crucial questions . . . freedom for whom, in practice? and from what, to do what?" (p. 11) are: 'In practice, and even in theory, for me and my fellow Radicals; from almost any restraints; and to suppress any but the mildest dissent from anything which we choose to say, and rule to be important.'

Over the Huntington affair at the University of Sussex Arblaster is, like C.A.F.D., in favour of the aims if not exactly the methods of the disruptors (pp. 168-70). The official C.A.F.D. statement blamed both the university authorities and the Sussex Indo-China Solidarity Committee: the former for having no proper machinery for preventing or withdrawing an invitation to lecture; the latter for going ahead with plans to stop that lecture after an inquorate union meeting: "At that point they put themselves in the position of arrogating to a minority the right to exclude views from the university" (*T.H.E.S.*, 15 June 1973).

Arblaster does eventually jib at the physical assault on Professor H. J. Eysenck (pp. 166-7), who has since been put at the top of the N.U.S. black list of forbidden speakers. Nevertheless, Eysenck's inquiries do "provide ammunition for white racialists", and more may "be needed to discredit them than learned articles in . . . minority journals" (p. 167). Such determination to discredit unwelcome findings unexamined scarcely consists with the C.A.F.D.'s promise "to nurse scepticism and to apply it to established beliefs" (quoted, p. 20). Furthermore, as any inquirer may easily discover, and as we ourselves saw in Chapter 5, Eysenck is not in fact a racist. He consistently repudiates any discrimination for or against any individual on the irrelevant grounds of their membership of a particular racial group. He is also absolutely clear on the logical point that racism neither is nor is entailed by any belief in average differences in ability and inclination between such groups. So, if either Arblaster or the militants of the N.U.S. really wanted to know, they could learn from him, both something of what the facts may be, and that these facts are not racism. And so might the many less activist members of possible audiences whom the new socialist, but not National Socialist, stormtroopers of the campus will not allow to listen.

(iv) Having laid so much stress upon rational, conscientious and truth-concerned inquiry as the moral foundation for academic freedoms, I want to put on show a piece of work published in the other Penguin Education Special mentioned in the present chapter. I should say at once that the disputed issue in 'the Arblaster Affair', much mentioned in *Academic Freedom* and elsewhere, was the failure of the University of Manchester to appoint the eponymous focus of that affair to a permanent Lectureship in Philosophy.

The work to be displayed begins with a quotation from what is by common consent one of the most important as well as the most entertaining philosophical articles to appear since the Second World War. This quotation reads: "our common stock of words embodies all the distinctions men have found worth drawing, and the connexions they have found worth making, in the lifetimes of many generations: these surely are likely to be more numerous, more sound . . . and more subtle . . . than any other that you or I are likely to think up in our armchairs of an afternoon" (Austin: 1, p. 130: as quoted by Arblaster, in Rubinstein and Stoneman, p. 36).

The two clauses which Arblaster is thus careful to replace by dots read: "since they have stood up to the long test of the survival of the fittest"; and "at least in all ordinary and reasonably practical matters". What he does quote then provides occasion for contemptuous comment: "To others of us it is at least equally reasonable to think that new and unfamiliar experiences or ways of seeing the world and human nature may require the formulation of new concepts and new theories, rather than efforts to cram them into old and established categories. Yet it has been left to 'outsiders' like Ernest Gellner (in *Words and Things*, 1959) and Herbert Marcuse (in *One-Dimensional Man*, 1964) to expose the conservatism of the linguistic orthodoxy in philosophy; and their criticisms have generally been ignored or treated with patronage or contempt by the 'professionals' in the field" (Rubinstein and Stoneman, pp. 36-7: reservation and sneer quotes original).

Yes indeed, there certainly has been a bit of ignoring going on; and some treating with patronage and contempt too. You may even talk about a "certain standard of honesty in the treatment of evidence"; so long, that is, as you do not concede that that displayed here is "obviously desirable". Anyone sufficiently interested in either fairness or philosophy to read a mere three further short pages of Austin will find on the third of these the gloss which Austin added to the two indicated omissions from Arblaster's quotation. This gloss reads: "Certainly ordinary language has no claim to be the last word. It embodies, indeed, . . . the inherited experience and acumen of many generations of men. . . . If a distinction works well for practical purposes . . . then there is sure to be something in it . . . yet this is likely enough not to be the best way of arranging things if our interests are more extensive and intellectual than the ordinary. And again . . . that experience has not been fed from the resources of the microscope and its successors. . . . Certainly, then, ordinary language is *not* the last word: in principle it can everywhere be supplemented and improved upon and superseded. Only remember, it *is* the *first* word". (Austin: 1, p. 133; italics his).

(v) One parenthetical observation deserves much more notice than Arblaster is prepared to give it: "The autonomy of institutions is being undermined . . . though perhaps it ought to be said that this subordination is far more complete in . . . Eastern Europe" (p. 145). Unfortunately this momentary insight is not allowed to intrude any element of balance into his perverse view of contemporary Britain. Nor is this, and the complementary observation that "Under normal conditions capitalism is not merely *compatible* with a limited liberal political system: it is directly *through* such a system that it survives . . ." (p. 25: italics his), permitted to raise any doubts about socialism. For, like so many of today's socialists, Arblaster dismisses all evidence of the actual effects of implementing Clause IV by insisting, for no reasons given, that socialism in practice is not socialism. The second passage previously omitted from the first quotation in the present paragraph reads: "what are sometimes described as the 'socialist' states of".

It is imperative, when a third or more of all mankind have for many years lived under Clause IV socialism, and while in none of these fully socialist countries is there even a pretence of a free press or of any respect for basic civil liberties, that all those socialists who really do still favour such freedoms should ask themselves, and tell others, what reason they have for assuming that in their own countries total socialism will in this vital respect be quite different. This uncomfortable yet urgent point is fiercely underlined if we notice that for frankly authoritarian socialists a main attraction of socialism seems to be precisely that in an economy wholly owned and controlled by the state there is and, it seems, can be no basis for opposition.

Ponder, for example, some words from a document entitled *The Falsifiers of Scientific Communism*, published in 1971 by the Institute of Marxism–Leninism in Moscow. It sketches a programme for the seizure of total and irremovable power by Communist Parties following 'united front' tactics: "Having once acquired political power, the working class implements the liquidation of the private ownership of the means of production. . . . As a result, under socialism, there remains no ground for the existence of any opposition parties counterbalancing the Communist Party" (see *The Economist*, 17 June 1972, p. 23). The monopoly socialist party does not, of course, have to be called a Communist Party.

(vi) Finally, someone with Arblaster's shortfused zeal to unmask unstated interests, and to see sinister motives behind stated reasons, might have been expected (prescriptive) to tell his readers that Steven Rose – commended for labours to prevent defence research in British universities (pp. 55ff.) – is a member of the Communist Party (Muscovite). For everyone knows, though too many are today too shy to say, why members of that party, and indeed the rest of the far left also, are eager to liquidate all Western defences. In general, and in conclusion, we have to insist that while Marxist–Leninists of various stripes remain active in C.A.F.D. there is no call to be surprised that it is not always what it would sometimes like to seem. A Chinese proverb runs: 'Those who travel in opposite directions do not lay plans together.'

Notes

1. In Note 30 to his second contribution to *Knowledge and Control,* Bourdieu writes: "By making the formal lecture the type of teaching with the highest prestige, the French system of education encourages works of a certain kind and intellectual qualities of a certain kind, pre-eminent importance being attached to qualities of exposition. Consideration should be given to the question whether an institution such as the British lecture system is associated with other habits of thought and other values" (pp. 206-7).

It is a pity that no one was able to put Bourdieu onto R. M. Hare's essay 'A School for Philosophers'. This constitutes a more particular but parallel study not of "the British lecture system" but of the association of the Oxford tutorial system with what are indeed "other habits of thought and other values". It was published first in *Ratio* for 1960 (vol. II, no. 2), but is now more easily to be found in Hare (pp. 38-53).

Two sorts of work in this area of which I myself would like to see more are: first, investigations of what someone who went to such and such a university at such and such a past period would have been supposed to have studied, and how; and, second, inquiries into the influence of university syllabi in particular subjects on the development of these subjects themselves. Is it, for instance, really impossible to discover any more about the undergraduate academic activities of John Locke and David Hume than we are told in the excellent standard biographies by Maurice Cranston and E. C. Mossner? And how far have even the professional philosophers been inhibited in their understanding of certain classical predecessors by the institutional fact that British schools have been split by a great divide between the Arts side and the Science side?

2. In "the darkness of this time" it may perhaps be necessary to say that the Authorised Version is at Genesis 1: 27.

3. Compare here Nell Keddie, who refers to studies which "suggest that the processes by which pupils are categorized are not self-evident and point to an overlooked consequence of a differentiated curriculum; that it is part of the process by which educational deviants are created and their deviant identities maintained" (p. 133).

4. The Cambridge anthropologist Edmund Leach contributed an

exercise for the application of the insights of the preceding Subsection (iv) in the third of his Reith Lectures: "Admittedly the statistics show a numerical increase in the incidence of crime. But this is a measure of police efficiency, not of the moral state of the nation. Crimes are created by Parliament; it needs a policeman to make a criminal" (*Listener,* 30 November 1967).

5. It is slightly comic as well as instructive that, immediately after one of his habitual sneers at "the prevailing 'liberal' orthodoxies", Young should speak, with no quotes now to express qualms about their standing, of "new knowledge areas such as the social sciences" (p. 23). On the whole subject of the logical relations or lack of relations between physiological causes, reasons as grounds, and reasons as motives, see my contribution to Smythies. I hope in the not-too-distant future to be able to produce a collection under the title *A Rational Animal* including revised versions of, among others, both this and Flew: 3.

6. I am not saying that there are more similarities than that indicated explicitly in the text. Certainly Young chose as a motto for the whole book a poem which begins by describing the pelican–egg–pelican cycle, and concludes with an anti-conservationist moral: "This sort of thing can go on/a very long time,/if you don't make an omelette" (p. viii). Again, we have Nell Keddie's apparent rejection of the ideal of a pupil "who can perceive and rationally evaluate alternatives". He will, she opines, become "the ideal man of a society which embraces consensus politics and a convergence theory of social class" (p. 137). Yet such scant and scattered hints are not, I think, expressions of considered personal commitments to revolution. It is just unthinking osmosis from the dominant sociological environment.

7. Compare the revealing meditations of Michael Drake of the Open University. As the newly appointed Dean of the Faculty of Social Sciences he is reviewing his previous experience at Kent. He takes note of the findings of a survey showing that students there did not even claim to do more than 33 hours a week academic work in term time, 16 hours a week in 9 of the weeks of their vacations, and none at all in the remaining 13 vacation weeks of the year. Drake proposes to draw a lesson: "Another reason for our failure to devise a satisfactory course was our unwillingness to tailor it to the time our students were prepared to spend on it". This statement, which deserves much wider publicity, is to be found in Vesey, pp. 84-5.

8. Young, for instance, apparently associates himself with the statement "that the dominant emphasis of the education systems of capitalist societies . . . the competitive concern with exams, grades and degrees, can be seen as one expression of the principles of a market economy" (p. 28). In Cox and Dyson: 2, Tibor Szamuely, who before escaping to Reading was himself educated and later taught in Socialist

Bloc countries, insisted that the facts are: both that their educational systems are far more ferociously competitive than ours; and that it is harder for those from disadvantaged homes to overcome their handicap there than it is here (pp. 53-6, especially p. 55 column 2).

9. Generally we must be on guard not to drain our words of meaning by removing the possibility of significant contrast. It cannot make sense to say that all language is in fact theoretical unless some conceivably might not be. Again, Ioan Davies writes: "the study of educational systems allows us to see what is ideological, to judge how information is distorted by the combined historical–structural conditions which determine how it is absorbed or rejected by the ideology of the system." Fair enough, perhaps. But if that is what he wanted to say he should not have started the sentence, as he did, by asserting: "All knowledge is shrouded in ideology" (Young, p. 282). Nor should he have said earlier, as if this were almost true by definition, that "education is as much about the *creation* of ideologies as it is about anything else" (p. 269: his italics). For it would not even make sense to speak of unmasking ideological distortions except in so far as it is possible to contrast these with some less distorted picture of the objective truth. This fundamental point, which seems not to have been fully grasped by our new Marxisant sociologico-critics, was well appreciated by Marx and Engels (Engels and Marx, pp. 23-4, 36-7 and 63-4).

10. Some would go further, and urge that certain Departments of Sociology could, if only they would, make a notable contribution to the solution of the second of these two social problems by simply shutting up shop. But it would obviously be an unbalanced exaggeration to suggest that the same prescription could effect any significant improvement in the first case.

11. I take this opportunity to add my voice to that of Robert Nisbet in urging that this and other works printed in the Everyman along with *The Social Contract* should be rearranged into their order of composition: it is especially sad that this was not done when this most widely used edition was reset and repaginated in 1956. The point, which Nisbet develops in an article in *Encounter* for September 1974, is that the chronological is in this case also the logical order of the development of the main themes in Rousseau's thought.

12. *The Republic,* §§ 451C ff. Later Plato falls from grace by making "the spirit of freedom and equal rights in the relation of men to women and women to men" one count in his indictment of democracy (§ 563 B).

13. It is unfortunate, especially in an examination of Marxism–Leninism in practice, that Lane uses the word 'democracy' in a way which carries no implication that it is possible to vote office-holders out. For it is in left-wing circles today, even among those who would if

pressed still claim to be in that quite different interpretation democrats, common for such grotesque phrases as 'Communist and other democratic forces' to be allowed to pass without either open protest or even any felt sense of scandal.

14. Since such sterilisation would in no way impair sexual activity I myself construe this as a proposal to reward low I.Q. Whether you agree on this point or not, you must allow that it was not Shockley but some of his Leeds opponents who were supporting discrimination on purely racial grounds. For his proposal, as reported by David Hencke (*T.H.E.S.*, 23 February 1973), contained no reference to colour. It was nevertheless abominated as racist by the student politicians of Leeds, apparently for no better reason than that there are in the United States "approximately six times as many Negroes as whites . . . classified as mentally retarded by traditional criteria" (Jensen, p. 241). By the way, Shockley is no kind of social scientist but a physicist. His shared Nobel Prize was for work in the development of the transistor.

15. Those whose political memories stretch back as far as the thirties and forties will find it wryly fitting that the name of Judy Bernal appears in a list of founder members of a new group of Radical scientists campaigning against Jensen (Richardson and Spears, p. 9). For while the protestant-trained Etonian J. B. S. Haldane finally broke with the Communist Party over the Lysenko affair, the Jesuit-schooled J. D. Bernal never for one moment wavered in his convert Stalinist obedience.

16. In a note in *Philosophy* vol. 49, no. 187 (1974) O. A. Ladimeji asked of this remark: "Is this an intimation of a massive attempt to sterilize a large part of the black working-class 'in the interest of the black people' and of equivalent parts of the white working-class 'in their true interests' also?" Since the possible problem is one of a genetic decline of American blacks relative to American whites, if anyone had been proposing policies, as I was not, he would, surely, have been silly to suggest action designed to affect (parts of) both groups in exactly the same way. Ladimeji's question is an example of the exploitation of racial tensions in the interests of class war.

17. I salute Donald McIntyre, of the University of Stirling, who recently developed a similar but slightly weaker and less philosophical thesis: "that assessment – is an integral part of effective teaching, and that attacks upon examinations as such have often been misdirected". I do this with the more pleasure because McIntyre's essay appeared in another Penguin Education Special of which I have harsh words to say (Rubinstein and Stoneman, p. 164). Its general tone and intellectual quality is fairly indicated in the first paragraph of the Introduction: "Throughout history the middle and upper classes . . . have given to the working classes as little and as poor an education as possible." All

that is offered by way of support for this extremely drastic and general thesis is a quotation from a "late Victorian ... former education minister". His statement concludes the paragraph: " 'what was wanted was to give to the children of the working man a sound, a compact, and a thorough education in those subjects which children during the limited time they were at school could master' " (p. 7). To support a characteristically venomous Radical charge that the class enemy have all always done, within no doubt whatever they perceived as the limits of possibility, the worst they could, we are given only the statement of one former minister in one country suggesting that his aim was to do, within what he perceived as the limits of the possible, the very best he could. The evidence cited thus not merely does not support the charge. It tends, as far as it goes, to disprove it.

18. For statements of these non-philosophical reasons see, for instance, C. B. Cox in *Encounter* for April 1973; the successive *Black Papers*, passim; and Arthur Pollard in Boyson.

19. For the non-specialist the best approach to Popper is perhaps through Magee's short essay in the Modern Masters series, and so on to personal selections from Popper: 1, 2 and 3.

20. It pains the liberal to discover that this phrase, which an earlier generation associated with Imperial Germany, is to be found in the *Nicomachean Ethics*. For Aristotle it was, apparently, just obvious "that what the law does not command, it forbids" (1138 A7).

21. The reference is to a ukase that such students were to pay much heavier university fees than their British-based contemporaries. There was at the time much protest against both the matter and manner of his intervention; and the University of Oxford, so long as its private endowment funds permitted, refused to practise this discrimination. Apart from its appeal to a narrow nationalism, Crosland's decision was clearly grounded also in international socialist principles. For the students likely to feel this imposition most, and perhaps to be kept away, must be those dependent on private resources rather than on governments.

22. The reference is to the steps taken by the 1964-70 Labour governments to ensure that the recommendations of the Boundary Commissioners should not be implemented. This Boundary Commission was set up, and its terms of reference laid down, with all-party agreement, under the 1945-51 Labour governments. The later Labour revulsion against such proposals springs from awareness that the directions of the continuing population movements of the last twenty or more years are such as to ensure that any impartial redistricting must result in the amalgamation, and hence the reduction, of some of Labour's electoral strongholds – particularly some inner-city pocket

boroughs which are now minute when compared with other suburban growth constituencies.

23. On these differences and similarities compare the *Report on the Committee on Relations with Junior Members* – 'the Hart Report' (Oxford: Oxford University Press, 1969; §§ 29ff.).

24. Keele had always been, and remains, in the van of redbrick universities in the proportion of its Senate constituted by elected representatives of junior faculty. But when a year or so earlier I had tried to get the institution of the Departmental Meeting, as a meeting of all full-time teaching members of the department, officially recognised, I failed even to find a seconder in Senate. After the troubles had begun, and when the call for student representation on everything became the trend, many Heads of Department, including some who had always been and still remained reluctant to treat their faculty juniors as colleagues and partners, became eager advocates for the proposals of this Majority Report.

25. In recent years the demand from student representatives has always been for greater weight on continuous assessment as opposed to final examination, and for more theses as opposed to question papers. It would be easier to believe in the untapped wealth of relevant experience if only these advocates started by recognising two obvious and fundamental points: that to allow work done early in a course to provide more than a safety net below those few who collapse in finals, must tend to pull down academic late developers and early sowers of wild oats; and that any increase in the weighting of work not done in examination conditions increases the incentives to cheat. Also, unless the continuous assessment is through a series of premature final examinations the grading is bound to be rather less reliable than where there is – as sometimes, admittedly there is not – a routine for the independent appraisal of all scripts by more than one assessor, and for an active external examiner to rule in any disagreements.

Anyone inclined to jettison the safeguards of the examination hall should study, for instance, Irving Babow's 'Academic Fraud' (*New Society*, 10 August 1972): the illicit provision of term papers and other forms of minithesis must be North America's number one growth point in the service sector. Stubborn innocence is, of course, also found among those with the age and experience which should have taught them better. I treasure the confession of Anthony King, Professor of Politics in the University of Essex: "The other day I was marking the project of a student I had never heard of: he had never been in one of my classes and I don't know him personally. But there the evidence was on paper: he was absolutely first class, someone I would have recommended without qualification for graduate work or to an employer looking for certain qualities of intellect" (*Spectator*, 6 June

1970). In the following issue I asked: "But just how does Mr. King know that the man he is prepared to recommend on the basis of his excellent work, who has never been in one of his classes, and whom he does not know personally, did in fact originate that work, especially since, on Mr. King's own account, these are 'pieces of work . . . which they would have done on their own largely without supervision' (ibid., 13 June 1970). I was not surprised that answer came there none. But those thinking of appointing Essex graduates, beware!

26. 'Academic Freedom: A Reply to Dr. Brown': I thank the author for giving me a copy of this so far unpublished paper.

27. I may mention that I had at one time hoped to include in the present volume at least the second part of a paper on 'Academic Freedoms as Means to the Ends of a University'. This was first published in *Universitas*, the Inter-Faculty Journal of the University of Ghana (vol. III, no. 1, October 1973), by people who have known something of real struggles for academic freedoms. The first part of that article covers similar ground to that of Chapter 5, above; the second was the text of the address which I gave to the annual ceremony of re-dedication to the ideals of academic freedom in Rhodes University, Grahamstown in 1967. I remarked that the contents of this address, including references to my then recent experiences in Poland and in Malawi, should be for some Radical demonstrators in Britain and the United States as pointed and relevant as they were for the officers of the South African Special Branch who were, as usual, most ostentatiously present at that Grahamstown occasion.

28. That this book does in general maintain the illiberal socialist orthodoxies of Penguin Education is indicated by Rubinstein's own conclusion: "Without absorbing the independent, and particularly the public schools, into the state system, any talk of education for democracy remains a mockery" (p. 88).

The hostility to streaming comes out most sharply in papers by Dennis Marsden and Brian Simon. In the former, revealingly entitled 'The Comprehensive School: Labour's Equality Machine', Marsden reassures himself "that the narrowly meritocratic emphasis on streaming and academic results . . . will be a temporary phase" and soon "the internal dynamic of reorganization should begin to assert itself" (p. 139). "These early disappointments for egalitarians emphasize that the community and the meritocratic schools represent quite different ideals . . . meritocrats and egalitarians will want to evaluate education, even the 'development of talent', by different criteria" (p. 140).

After digesting this those who think of education as a matter of learning, rather than as an engine of equalisation – those, that is, who are in Penguinspeak meritocrats rather than egalitarians – may be pleased to find in 'Streaming and Unstreaming in the Secondary

School' Simon's statement: "It cannot be too strongly pointed out that the abolition of streaming is in no sense linked with complacency about academic standards" (p. 148). But to be pleased here would be to be deceived. For Simon gives the game away later on the same page: "One problem is that of the criteria by which the change is to be evaluated, since the abolition of streaming means the substitution of different aims from those of the past." He does not spell out what these different aims are: such reserve is, perhaps, discreet.

29. H. J. Eysenck, as we saw in Chapter 5, certainly is not in the obnoxious normative sense a racialist (Eysenck, pp. 9-11 and passim). Nor can that other favourite enemy, the Monday Club, be said either to reject the true democrat's insistence that it must always be possible "to vote the scoundrels out", or to be committed to depriving all their political opponents of basic civil liberties.

30. When I appeared in Capital Radio and Thames T.V. discussions of the N.U.S. embargo all but one of the N.U.S. official spokesmen, including Steve Parry, were on their own account either members or fellow-travellers of that party. The sole exception was the then President, who claimed to be an independent left-wing socialist. The appointed representative of C.A.F.D., a faculty member from the Department of Sociology in the Polytechnic of North London, who shared in the first of these two programmes, was also a party member. For good measure so is Steven Rose, Professor of Biology in The Open University, who tried but narrowly failed to win full support for this N.U.S. policy at a specially convened C.A.F.D. conference. The conference was, however, equally reluctant to go along with the National Council for Civil Liberties in actual opposition (*T.H.E.S.*, 3 May 1974). Those who wish to stay comfortably in the swim, unable to deny yet refusing to give any weight to this evidence, will now with a sneer or a giggle utter the thought-stopping cliché 'reds under the bed' (Flew: 7, 4.23 and 5.1).

Bibliography

This is intended to cover all, but only, the works referred to in the text, the aim being to produce an adequately full and precise, but economical and unobtrusive, system for reference.

ARBLASTER, A., *Academic Freedom* (Harmondsworth and Baltimore: Penguin, 1974).

ARISTOTLE, *Nicomachean Ethics*, trans. H. Rackham (London and New York: Heinemann and Putnam, 1926).

AUSTIN, J. L.:

   1 *Philosophical Papers*, ed. J. O. Urmson and G. J. Warnock (Oxford: Clarendon Press, 1961).

   2 *Sense and Sensibilia*, ed. G. J. Warnock (Oxford: Clarendon Press, 1962).

   3 *How To Do Things with Words*, ed. J. O. Urmson (Oxford: Clarendon Press, 1962).

AYER, A. J.:

   1 *Language, Truth and Logic*, 2nd ed. (London: Gollancz, 1946).

   2 *The Foundations of Empirical Knowledge* (London: Macmillan, 1940).

BERG, C., *Deep Analysis* (London: Allen & Unwin, 1946).

BERLIN, I., *Historical Inevitability* (London: Oxford University Press, 1954).

BETEILLE, A. (ed.), *Social Inequality* (Harmondsworth and Baltimore: Penguin, 1969).

BLACKBURN, R. (ed.), *Ideology in Social Science* (London: Collins Fontana, 1972).

BOUDON, R.:

   1 *The Logic of Sociological Explanation,* trans. T. Burns (Harmondsworth: Penguin, 1969).

   2 *Education, Opportunity, and Social Inequality* (New York: Wiley, 1974).

BOYSON, R. (ed.), *The Accountability of Schools* (London: Churchill, 1973).

COCKBURN, A., and BLACKBURN, R. (eds), *Student Power* (Harmondsworth and Baltimore: Penguin, 1969).

COLLINGWOOD, R. G., *An Autobiography* (Harmondsworth: Penguin, 1944).

CONFUCIUS (K'UNG FU-TZU), *The Analects,* trans. and ed. W. E. Soothill (Taiyuanfu, Shansi: Soothill, 1910).

COX, C. B., and DYSON, A. E. (eds):

  1 *Fight for Education: A Black Paper* (London: *Critical Quarterly,* 1969).

  2 *Black Paper Two* (London: *Critical Quarterly,* 1970).

  3 *Black Paper Three* (London: *Critical Quarterly,* 1971).

ENGELS, F., and MARX, K., *The German Ideology,* ed. S. Ryazanskaya, no translator named (Moscow: Progress, 1964).

EVANS-PRITCHARD, E. E., *Witchcraft, Oracles and Magic among the Azande* (Oxford: Clarendon Press, 1937).

EYSENCK, H. J., *Race, Intelligence and Education* (London: Temple Smith, 1971).

FLEW, A. G. N.:

  1 *Hume's Philosophy of Belief* (London and New York: Routledge & Kegan Paul and Philosophical Library, 1961).

  2 *God and Philosophy* (London and New York: Hutchinson and Harcourt Brace, 1966).

  3 'A Linguistic Philosopher Looks at Lenin's *Materialism and Empirio-Criticism*', in *Praxis* (Zagreb, 1967).

  4 *An Introduction to Western Philosophy* (London and Indianapolis: Thames & Hudson and Bobbs-Merrill, 1971).

  5 *Crime or Disease?* (London and New York: Macmillan and Barnes & Noble, 1973).

  6 *The Presumption of Atheism* (London: Pemberton, 1975).

  7 *Thinking about Thinking* (London: Fontana, 1975).

GEYL, P., *Debates with Historians* (London: Batsford, 1955).

HARE, R. M., *Essays on Philosophical Method* (London: Macmillan, 1971).

HERRNSTEIN, R. J., *IQ in the Meritocracy* (New York: Atlantic Monthly, 1973).

HESLEP, R. D. (ed.), *Philosophy of Education 1971* (Edwardsville, Ill.: Philosophy of Education Society).

HIRST, P., *Knowledge and the Curriculum* (London: Routledge & Kegan Paul, 1974).

HUDSON, W. D. (ed.), *The Is/Ought Question* (London: Macmillan, 1969).

HUXLEY, A., *Brave New World* (London: Chatto & Windus, 1952 reprint).

JENCKS, C., and others, *Inequality* (London: Allen Lane, 1973).

JENSEN, A. R., *Genetics and Education* (Edinburgh: Constable, 1972).

JONES, O. R. (ed.), *The Private Language Argument* (London: Macmillan, 1971).

KAFKA, F., *The Trial,* trans. W. and E. Muir (Harmondsworth: Penguin, 1953).

KANT, I.:

1 *Critique of Pure Reason,* trans. N. Kemp Smith (London: Macmillan, 1929).

2 *A Critique of Judgement,* trans. J. G. Meredith (Oxford: Clarendon Press, 1952).

KUHN, T., *The Structure of Scientific Revolutions* (Chicago: Chicago University Press, 1962).

LAKATOS, I., and MUSGRAVE, A. (eds), *Criticism and the Growth of Knowledge* (Cambridge: Cambridge University Press, 1970).

LANE, D., *The End of Inequality? Stratification under State Socialism* (Harmondsworth and Baltimore: Penguin, 1971).

LENIN, V. I., *Materialism and Empirio-Criticism,* no translator named (Moscow: Foreign Languages Publishing House, 1952).

MAGEE, B., *Popper* (London: Fontana, 1973).

MAO TSE-TUNG, *Quotations from Chairman Mao,* no translator named (Peking: Foreign Languages Press, 1966).

MOORE, G. E., *Philosophical Studies* (London: Routledge & Kegan Paul, 1922).

MUIRHEAD, J. H. (ed.), *Contemporary British Philosophy,* First Series (London: Allen & Unwin, 1925).

ORWELL, G., *1984* (London: Secker & Warburg, 1949).

PARSONS, T., and CLARK, K. B. (eds), *The Negro American* (Cambridge, Mass.: Houghton Mifflin, 1966).

PLATO, *The Republic,* trans. P. Shorey (Cambridge, Mass., and London: Harvard University Press and Heinemann, 1966).

POPPER, K. R.:

1 *The Open Society,* 5th ed. (London: Routledge & Kegan Paul, 1966).

2 *The Logic of Scientific Discovery* (London: Hutchinson, 1959).

3 *Conjectures and Refutations* (London: Routledge & Kegan Paul, 1963).

RICHARDSON, K., and SPEARS, D. (eds), *Race, Culture and Intelligence* (Harmondsworth: Penguin, 1972).

ROUSSEAU, J.-J., *The Social Contract, etc.,* trans. and ed. G. D. H. Cole (New York and London: Dutton and Dent, 1910: all references are to the new 1956 pagination).

RUBINSTEIN, D., and STONEMAN, C. (eds), *Education for Democracy,* 2nd ed. (Harmondsworth and Baltimore: Penguin, 1972).

RYLE, G.:

1 *The Concept of Mind* (London: Hutchinson, 1949).

2 *Plato's Progress* (Cambridge: Cambridge University Press, 1966).

SCHEFFLER, I., *The Language of Education* (Springfield, Ill.: Charles Thomas, 1960).

Sjöstrand, W., *Freedom and Equality* (Stockholm: Foreningen för Svensk Undervisningshistoria, 1973).

Skolimowski, H., *Polish Analytical Philosophy* (London: Routledge & Kegan Paul, 1967).

Smythies, J. R. (ed.), *Brain and Mind* (London and New York: Routledge & Kegan Paul and Humanities Press, 1965).

Solzhenitsyn, A., *The Gulag Archipelago*, trans. T. P. Whitney (London: Fontana, 1974).

Trigg, R., *Reason and Commitment* (Cambridge: Cambridge University Press, 1973).

Vesey, G. (ed.), *The Proper Study* (London: Macmillan, 1971).

Waley, A. (trans.), *One Hundred and Seventy Chinese Poems* (London: Constable, 1918).

Waugh, E., *Scoop* (Harmondsworth: Penguin, 1963).

Williams, R., *George Orwell* (London: Fontana, 1971).

Williams, R. (ed.), *May Day Manifesto 1968* (Harmondsworth: Penguin, 1968.)

Wilson, B. (ed.), *Rationality* (Oxford: Blackwell, 1970).

Winch, P., *The Idea of a Social Science* (London: Routledge & Kegan Paul, 1958).

Wittgenstein, L., *Philosophical Investigations*, trans. G. E. M. Anscombe (Oxford: Blackwell, 1953).

Young, Michael, *The Rise of the Meritocracy* (London: Thames & Hudson, 1958; Pelican ed., 1961).

Young, M. F. D. (ed.), *Knowledge and Control* (London: Collier-Macmillan, 1971).

Index of Personal Names

This is intended to cover all, but only, the names of non-fictitious persons occurring in the text (pp. 1–128) and in the notes (pp. 129–36).

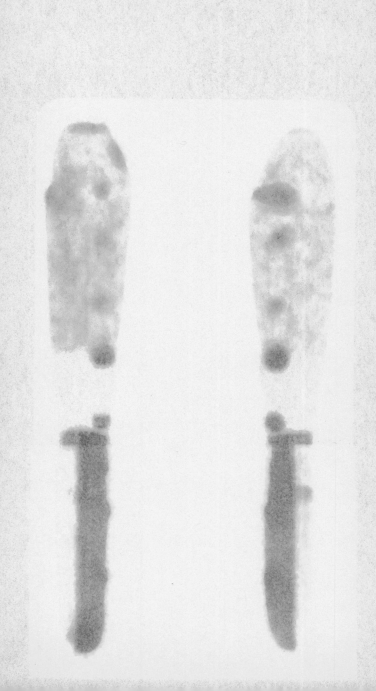